# In My EXPERT Opinion...

## Becoming an
# Effective Expert
### in the
## Financial Services Industry

# MICHAEL D. WEINER, J.D.

LUMINARE PRESS

WWW.LUMINAREPRESS.COM

Printed in the United States of America

Cover Design: Melissa Lund

Luminare Press
438 Charnelton St., Suite 101
Eugene, OR 97401
www.luminarepress.com

LCCN: 2018960095
ISBN: 978-1-64388-019-8

*To my wife,*
*Kathy Davis-Weiner,*
*for her support and for being there*
*when I, so often, was not.*

Drawing on his deep experience, Michael Weiner has written one of the very best "how to" books on the market for would-be expert witnesses. His timeless and invaluable tips, passed on in an engaging and very accessible style, will be essential reading for anyone thinking about hanging out their shingle as an expert witness

—DONALD S. DAVIDSON, SHAREHOLDER
Greenberg Traurig, LLP

Mr. Weiner draws on his extensive experience to provide a great introduction to the world of financial service litigation from the perspective of the expert witness. All litigants—both plaintiffs and defendants—would be better served if experts lived by Mr. Weiner's fourteen essential rules. His book is a must read for any financial services professional looking to transition from working in the industry to testifying about the industry.

—KENNETH F. BERG, PARTNER
Ulmer & Berne LLP

Michael Weiner writes "The purpose of these materials is to use my background to guide the prospective expert from 'subject matter expert' to 'expert witness.'" There is in fact a considerable gap between the two, and his book will help readers navigate the crossing. This should be required reading not only for experts old and new, but also for lawyers who retain experts in the field of financial services industry litigation. Highly recommended!

—ROBERT S. BANKS JR.,
Banks Law Office, P.C.

When it comes to knowing what it takes to be a consistently effective expert witness, Michael Weiner is an expert. There are valuable lessons in this book for even the most experienced testifying expert; for those who are not yet seasoned in the courtroom, it is an indispensable how-to guide, full of practical "do's and don'ts" that are illustrated, often amusingly, with anecdotes from the author's abundant personal experience. In addition, any lawyer who uses experts in his or her cases will do well to read and heed the sound advice that appears on every page.

—LLOYD S. CLAREMAN, ATTORNEY AT LAW
New York, N.Y.


Michael Weiner's book In My Expert Opinion is a must read for the novice expert witness, as well as the more experienced one. Chock full of specific suggestions for how to prepare to be an outstanding expert and how to obtain and project confidence and know how, this book is invaluable for its practical nitty gritty guidelines—including how to deal with billing, how to build and maintain one's reputation, how to speak in simple, relatable language, and how to prepare for, deal with and even relish cross examination.

—ROBERT SHLACHTER, SHAREHOLDER
Stoll Berne Lokting & Shlachter

# CONTENTS

# FOREWORD

Experienced trial attorneys and sophisticated clients know that an expert witness can make – or break – a case. They also know that a stellar expert witness – one who is not only incredibly knowledgeable, discerning, credible, candid, articulate, persuasive and likeable, but also 100% honest and straightforward – is worth every dollar that the expert charges for the services provided.

Over the past several decades, Michael Weiner has established that he is not merely a stellar expert witness, but also one of the most sought after experts in the financial services industry. I know this from personal experience; after Michael retired from his expert witness practice, I implored Michael to testify for me one final time despite his retirement. In his typical gracious manner, Michael agreed to do so and he was in court when the federal court jury was empaneled in the class action lawsuit that we were defending and about to try. The class action, which involved a municipal bond offering that went into default, needed strong, experienced experts, and we had that in spades with Michael on our side.

The enthusiasm, dedication, knowledge and expertise that Michael brought to his cases for over 20 years as an expert witness are manifest in Michael's *In My Expert Opinion: Becoming an Expert in the Financial Services Industry*. This book is a must-read for any aspiring – or experienced – expert witness, as well as for lawyers, arbitrators, educators and law students who are interested in how to "do it right." Indeed, my only quibble with Michael's excellent book is its title (which perhaps should include four additional words, post-ellipses): "*Becoming* – and Remaining Relevant as – *an Expert in the Financial Services Industry.* This is so because Michael's practical, common sense approach to being an expert witness does not apply solely to newbies; Michaels' compilation of advice interspersed with his "lessons learned" (titled "Personal Asides") can and should be embraced by every expert witness, whether seasoned or aspiring, because doing so will make any expert witness a better expert witness.

Expert witnesses are sometimes referred to derogatorily as "hired guns" who will say just about anything – whether they believe it or not – to cater to the preferences or requirements of the party who hires them. While the label may indeed be apt for a very small percentage of witnesses who called themselves "experts," such witnesses do not deserve the expert appellation and they are not the intended audience for Michael's book. Indeed, such "experts" will in all likelihood quickly be revealed for what they are, and their foray into the expert witness realm will undoubtedly be short-lived. Michael – and other respected experts with staying power and impeccable reputations – are the antithesis of those who bring derision to the expert witness field.

True expert witnesses such as Michael are essential to the proper functioning of our legal system, and their essential mission is simple: to assist the fact-finder in getting to the truth. One need look no further than to Michael's "ESSENTIAL RULE NUMBER ONE: Never lose sight of your integrity; maintain your independence" to surmise that the advice, insights and lessons provided by Michael in his book are predicated on the same qualities that we universally value: honesty, integrity, professionalism, diligence, expertise, respect for others, and uncompromised ethics. In his informative, compelling and sometimes humorous (self-deprecating) book, Michael presents a practical, logical, step-by-step roadmap of what to expect, how to get started, how to act, how not to act, how to prepare, how to testify and how to succeed. Importantly, but not surprisingly, "doing it right" (my words) with integrity is the recurring building block/theme for success in Michael's book. That is how Michael conducted himself his entire career.

Experienced trial attorneys know that their demeanor, conduct, mannerisms and words are being scrutinized by judges, juries or arbitrators from their first interaction through the end of the case. If an attorney's credibility is compromised, so too is the credibility of the attorney's client because the attorney projects – indeed embodies – the values of the client. In a similar manner, an expert witness reflects the core values of the expert's client. If the expert is not forthcoming with information, or takes objectively unjustifiable positions, or is arrogant, or is simply not likeable or worse, the client will suffer. Michael understands this and he gives cogent advice on how to be an effective expert witness without ever compromising one's ethics or duties.

Over the course of my 35-plus years of being a trial and arbitration attorney for most of the major Wall Street firms and for many others, I have had the pleasure and privilege of working with the best of the very best expert witnesses in the financial services industry, including Michael. Sadly, some of them have passed away or, like Michael, have retired. When the current bull market ends (as do all such runs), financial services firms will undoubtedly again see an uptick in claims filed against them by investors who will invariably claim that the losses they incurred resulted from wrongdoing by the financial services firms and their advisors (as opposed to market forces).

When that day arrives (and it will), those financial services firms will need talented – and ethical – expert witnesses to help their attorneys defend such claims. I can think of no better way for an aspiring expert witness to be inspired to greatness than to read Michael's book. The same holds true for experienced securities litigators and seasoned expert witnesses: reading Michael's book may well revitalize one's faith in the litigation process and renew one's appreciation of the skills, expertise and overall contributions that capable expert witnesses bring to the litigation team.

One final thought: Michael's book is a timely reminder that truth, respect, honor and integrity – though seemingly in short supply in the political realm and on social media – still matter, and indeed are more important than ever today. Those who heed Michael's advice and who embrace the principles that he espouses will substantially enhance their odds of being successful as expert witnesses, all the while benefitting the legal system by raising both the caliber of, and the expectations for, the next generation of expert witnesses.

Ben Suter
Shareholder
Keesal, Young & Logan
San Francisco, CA

# The Fourteen Essential Rules

**ESSENTIAL RULE NUMBER ONE:** Never lose sight of your integrity; maintain your independence.

**ESSENTIAL RULE NUMBER TWO:** Confidence never—ever—invites sarcasm or condescension.

**ESSENTIAL RULE NUMBER THREE:** On cross-examination, keep your answers short and simple.

**ESSENTIAL RULE NUMBER FOUR:** Always examine the premise of a cross-examination question and never answer a question that is improperly premised.

**ESSENTIAL RULE NUMBER FIVE:** Listen, understand, process, hesitate, and only then, speak.

**ESSENTIAL RULE NUMBER SIX:** No one should attempt to testify if there is even the slightest uncertainty regarding one's expertise in the subject matter of opinion testimony.

**ESSENTIAL RULE NUMBER SEVEN:** Practice, Practice, Practice Your Qualifications.

**ESSENTIAL RULE NUMBER EIGHT:** These Little Housekeeping Matters Are Your Lifeblood—Do It Right!

**ESSENTIAL RULE NUMBER NINE:** Always assume everything you write or otherwise prepare is discoverable and will be seen by opposing counsel.

**ESSENTIAL RULE NUMBER TEN:** Understanding and communicating the meaning of words on paper is not makeshift work; it is essential to your role. It **is** your role. This is how you become invaluable to counsel. Giving counsel insights that he or she could not otherwise acquire makes you a unique asset.

**ESSENTIAL RULE NUMBER ELEVEN:** Everything in your expert report that can be sourced, should have a footnote indicating that source. It will make your life infinitely easier at your deposition and at trial.

**ESSENTIAL RULE NUMBER TWELVE:** Every word of your expert report will be dissected; you must be prepared to be deposed and cross-examined on every word in your report. Therefore, write every word with extreme precision and care. Also, be prepared to defend alternatives, theories, or opinions omitted; they are fair game as well.

**ESSENTIAL RULE NUMBER THIRTEEN:** Critiquing the opposing expert is a critical job function. Counsel is relying on your expertise for an effective cross-examination. You have an implicit duty to relay to counsel your expert, in-depth analysis of the testimony and work product of the opposing expert.

**ESSENTIAL RULE NUMBER FOURTEEN:** You are a part of a legal process and have an implicit duty to understand that process, which includes reasonable deference to your counsel's preferences.

# CHAPTER ONE

# BACKGROUND AND THEORY

Being thrown into litigation as an expert witness without a guide, or even a guidebook, is like being asked to pitch in the World Series after a successful career as a college batting coach. Yes, you were in the same general field of work, yes, you were renowned, but the differences between batting and pitching, between college and the pros, are monumental—and the skill sets are only tangentially related.

To enter the profession of expert witness consulting and testimony in the financial services arena without a foundation in both what to expect and how to prepare for the challenges ahead will inevitably lead to the exposure of one's professional limitations, and perhaps an abrupt, and unnecessary, conclusion to an aspiring career.

Most aspiring expert witnesses in the financial services industry were tremendously successful in their careers, and are now looking to transition from being a batting coach into a starting pitcher. The stakes are enormous; not only are sizeable monetary sums involved, but there are personal and corporate reputations at stake, and the possibility of careers which might be forever impaired. Your contributions and testimony can literally be the difference between success and failure; counsel will be relying upon you to make a difference.

Therefore, as you undertake your expert witness assignment with gravity, and there is no other way, there is enormous pressure on you to perform in both an outstanding and professional manner. "Outstanding" refers to the quality of your work and your work product; "professional" refers to the methodology of delivery and working relationships. You will be expected to be an integral player in a highly critical matter. It is indeed the World Series.

The purpose of this book is to assist in that transition and to make you as successful in your new career as you were in your previous endeavors. It should also appeal to legal professionals who demand excellence because, among other things, their clients demand the best possible representation—and that clearly includes you in your role as an expert.

You will have to learn new skills and hone existing ones. You will have to learn to listen in greater depth and precision than in any other situation you have ever endured. You will have to learn to speak with clarity, brevity, and precision. You will have to learn to write with even greater precision than you will speak. You must learn to work with counsel and walk a precise line between interference and assistance. (Yes, there is indeed a theme: precision. You are embarking on a journey that demands laser-like precision in the written word, the spoken word, and the relationships that you must build). In short, you will have to internalize the nuances of a new professional world: litigation support.

*  *  *

**Note:** *I use the word "litigation" to include all manners of dispute resolution, including arbitration; technically, it is not completely accurate, but indulge me on this point.*

**Note (also):** *Most of my testimonial and consulting practice was on the defense side of the industry. I would defend broker-dealers, futures commission merchants, or individuals against charges of "securities fraud" in the broadest sense of the term. It would include allegations such as churning, mismanagement, unsuitable recommendations, negligence, misrepresentation, statutory and common-law fraud, and conflicts of interest. I have tried to write this book for the aspiring expert who will represent either the claimant (or plaintiff) or the respondent (or defendant), but many of my examples will, necessarily, be taken from a defense point of view. However, all my advice as to how to become an effective expert should be equally applicable to either "side of the table."*

The broad picture of arbitration and why it plays a central role in the dispute-resolution process in the financial services industry is found in the introductory pages of Chapter Seven of this book. In short, the industry was allowed to adopt the mandatory arbitration process through a Supreme Court decision in 1987 and has been using it almost exclusively ever since. Whether mandatory arbitration, or any form of arbitration at all, survives the reform push of the current regulators is yet to be seen, as the concept of mandatory arbitration is currently under attack.

But as it stands now, almost any retail client who has a dispute with a brokerage firm is effectively precluded from going to court and instead, the matter will be referred to the well-honed arbitration machinery found in "FINRA" (the Financial Industry Regulatory Association). There are other arbitration forums, such as JAMS (Judicial Arbitration Mediation Services) and AAA (American Arbitration Association), but most of securities matters are heard before FINRA.

A FINRA arbitration is somewhat like a trial; two sides with counsel are presenting evidence to a trier of fact—in this case three representatives of the public (or two public representatives and one industry representative) who are trained in the arbitration process and the basics of the industry. But it is less formal; it is held in a non-judicial setting without the trappings of a full trial. Arbitrators are allowed to, rather expected to, give a judgment which, if applicable, includes damages—and even punitive damages, if appropriate. The theory is that an arbitration will be faster and cheaper than a trial while maintaining the fairness and impartiality of a trial.

The role of the expert is to aid the trier of fact in understanding issues based on contested facts. The theory is that the field of financial services is complex (which it is), and arbitration panels need help (which they do). Experts are not new or unknown in litigation, but the use of experts in financial services arbitrations have grown from an occasional use in the 1980s to near mandatory today. Rarely will an arbitration with a considerable damage request go forward without expert opinions being offered by the Claimant (the functional equivalent of the Plaintiff). And if the Claimant has an expert, well, then so shall the Respondent (the functional equivalent of the Defendant). And so it evolved. The expert witness field in financial services was functionally created and it continues to grow.

Today, many a successful industry veteran, recently

retired or simply seeking an additional professional outlet, has hung out a shingle and declared that the expertise gained through years of industry practice makes one an expert. In theory it might do so, but it also takes significant work to get proficient.

**Becoming an expert witness is not an easy task.** There is a relatively steep learning curve. I learned by simply doing; there was no manual; no one told me the ins and the outs of expert witness testimony. Prior to joining The Bates Group (hereafter referred to as "Bates"), my experience as an expert had been limited to being called into disputes before judges in the federal courts in Chicago for technical explanations and interpretations of exchange rules when I was Counsel to the Chicago Mercantile Exchange. At Bates, when I asked about training to become an expert; i.e., what should I expect and how should I prepare, I was met with amused or blank stares and an admonition to go talk to counsel and read the case materials. (Not a bad start, but there is a bit more, a lot more, to this endeavor).

When I discovered that my partners were deliberately downplaying the industry rules and regulations as a basis for expert testimony, I found a whole new area in which to direct my energies and my testimony. Instead of simply presenting data, (for example, what happened in the account and how a reasonable broker or manager would look upon that data), I tackled the intersections of facts, data, law, custom and industry practice. It was new and exciting, not only to me, but also to the many attorneys whom I began to work with. And what I learned from my early years was that testimony is flexible. I can be as broad and deep or as narrow and focused as necessary to best serve my client; I can present data; I can create hypothetical situations; I can argue (or at least attempt to argue) the law; I can present professional research; I can do my own research; I can be creative in my presentations. Most importantly, I can adjust to the needs of the client and thus be a truly effective testifying expert in the field of financial services.

•  •  •

**A Personal Aside:** *An illustration of broad and deep was my state court testimony in White Plains, New York which lasted a grueling four full days. I was grilled by four of the best criminal defense attorneys in the country who were ruthless in their cross-examinations of me. My direct testimony was exhaustive, breaking new ground for me as an expert testifying to statistical methods and conclusions as well as enormous data files. The testimony was also challenging the ability of a jury to internalize complex theories and a huge amount of data.*

*An illustration of narrow and focused was my direct testimony in an arbitration in Fort Lauderdale, Florida, which consisted of one question verifying some data work my associates had prepared. But the cross-examination took about an hour and resulted in a newly minted junior attorney pleading with the arbitration chair: "But he won't answer my questions. He's being a weasel." (I was not a weasel, but, within my office, that became my new nickname.)*

Every individual expert witness who raises his or her right hand and swears to tell the truth before a judge, jury, or arbitration panel is, presumably, well-qualified in his or her own field. This book does not delve into that particular expertise; the subject matter expertise will already be presumed a given. Rather, the materials will aid in teaching how to become an effective testifying or consulting expert, which means that with a significant degree of time and experience, one can become a valued participant within counsel's team to assist the triers of fact better understand the issues at hand.

Your goal should always be to become invaluable to counsel, so that you become, within ethical boundaries, a trusted participant and someone upon whom counsel can rely. What are those ethical boundaries? That will be thoroughly discussed in a subsequent chapter, but in short, you must be a valued litigation participant without losing either your independence or your principles.

However, there is an inescapable progression. Until one proves himself or herself through one or more "baptisms of fire," i.e., through at least one full hearing or trial wherein you are battle-tested and you (and counsel) come out smiling, counsel will be wary of relying on any expert beyond those narrow issues upon which the expert was hired. What that means is until you are better known and respected, you will provide input and testimony regarding only your basic assignment, nothing more. That is both appropriate and predictable.

What that means from a practical standpoint is that initially, one should not expect to participate in strategy sessions, to help prepare witnesses, to make meaningful tactical suggestions, to write one's own direct examination or to formulate the cross-examination of the opposing expert. All of that may eventually come to pass after successful interactions with counsel—but it might take multiple passes with counsel and the entire counsel team for that to occur. Indeed, it might take years of experience. And, it goes without saying, that until one acquires a reputation that spreads across both law and securities firms, one will be continually proving oneself.

But upon successful completion of a significant task, be it testimony or consultation, your reputation will begin to build, multiple opportunities will present themselves, reliance will grow, and one will become a true expert: not just a subject matter expert, but a true asset to your client.

•  •  •

**Another Personal Aside:** *At one time, all the experts at The Bates Group were admonished not to refer to the opposing expert as an "**opposing** expert," but rather as the "**other** expert." That well-meaning caution was supposed to reflect the view that all experts are independent neutrals who do not "oppose" each other, but merely have differing professional opinions. That advice is praiseworthy, and certainly technically correct, but the reality is that both experts are there to express views that assist the triers of fact reach conclusions favorable to the clients who hired them. The difficulty is to balance that assistance with your ethical duty to be, in fact, independent and neutral.*

Expert work in the financial services industry is technical and complex. In its own way, it is as intricate as medical or engineering testimony. What the financial services expert needs as a basis for testimony is always rooted in his or her's experience in the industry. That experience is what will be the subject of an expert's *voir dire* (more on that later), and that is where you, as that expert, will convince the triers of fact that your opinions are solid, relevant, and ultimately, worthy of adoption.

It will also be tremendously helpful if you know the

bigger picture within the field of financial services without presuming to be an expert in everything financial. (More of that later in Essential Rule Number Six). Thus, if you are an expert in sales practices, you should also know the fundamentals of margining. If you are a margin expert, you should be familiar with the fundamentals of how the front office is run. If you are an expert in derivatives, you should have knowledge of how those issues are traded. If you are a supervisor, you should know the FINRA manual in sufficient depth to not be unnerved when opposing counsel questions you on a relevant section.

In other words, unless you are comfortable in a hyper-specialized role and can become the unique go-to individual offering opinions that virtually no one else can give, it is better to recognize and take advantage of the fact that your background includes context, and that context is important in the formulation of both opinions and testimony.

No, you need not be an expert in the law, nor any case law, even Supreme Court decisions. But as an industry expert, on either side of the table, you should present a well-rounded understanding of the financial industry, not merely the processes and procedures from the firm to which you were recently attached, so that you may speak to the alleged wrongdoings and the fundamentals of "customs and practices of the industry."

Thus, it is critical that you understand how your former competition would, at least on paper, handle the issues at hand. You have an obligation to be an "industry" expert, not just a "Firm XYZ" expert. From the plaintiff or claimant side, it is even more critical to be able to present context so that an opinion can be based on "customs and practices of the industry" as a whole.

Whichever side of the table you sit, memorize that phrase: "custom and practices of the industry." It is a mantra that you should soon be using often to give context to your testimony, but also be assured that it will frequently be used against you. It is the standard upon which many alleged violations are judged. Only if you can see and understand the bigger picture can you become an effective expert in the financial services industry.

For example, as a defense expert, you may very well be engaged in dialogue with opposing counsel on the application of a document vis-a-vis the Operations Manual to a particular firm. You should, and will, know how that document relates to the operations of that firm. But that is just the beginning.

An operations manual is not law; it is not even a FINRA rule (although it may very well reflect one), nor is it an exchange rule. What you must do is explain, from your own experience, how the industry operates, how that section of the manual reflects not only good internal procedure, but fits squarely into the policies and procedures of the industry itself. If the document goes above and beyond standard policy, so much the better—explain it. If it deviates from what you know as standard policy, make that distinction in a careful, thoughtful manner. But the key is to be broader than any one section of a manual or of a document reflected in that manual; you are an industry expert and the customs and practices of the industry as a whole are of immense value to a trier of fact who needs to know context. You are providing that necessary context.

*　*　*

**Caution:** As intimated above, If you are testifying for the defense, industry custom and practice can also be used against you. If you are defending a particularly odd set of facts, be prepared to have the term "custom and practices" thrown at you in the context of negligence; i.e., those facts, because they allegedly do not conform to the custom and practice of the industry allegedly also constitute a breach of some "duty." You might think of answering that line of attack in several ways: First, and the strongest argument is that you disagree that there is a lack of conformity with custom and practice. After all, you are the expert who best knows the industry, the whole industry, not just the practices of one firm. Second, refer to documentation: Get out the FINRA rules and/or the firm's compliance or operations manual, make the link between them, and then conclude that the rules and manuals show that the facts presented are perfectly in line with the regulatory requirements and those certainly trump any "custom and practice" argument.

"Duty" is a legal term which anchors the negligence concept. What you are really doing, subtly and without becoming too legalistic, is either denying that a "duty" exists, or assuring the trier of facts that any "duty" has been fulfilled. But never get bogged down in the argument as to whether a duty existed. That specified legal concept should be left to the lawyers, and indeed, if asked, expect your counsel to vehemently object to the question.

Personally, I look at "custom and practice" as a weak link; it is used when counsel has no legal or regulatory ammunition and must refer to more ethereal sources.

**You must be able to teach and explain the nuances of the industry.** Remember, juries know nothing about the field; judges may, or may not, have enough specialized knowledge of it to be able to put testimony into the proper context; and even arbitration panels may include public members who are not familiar with many of the industry mores. You must assume, until proven otherwise, that all testimony will be received with a grain of incomprehension—despite the robotic nods of approval you receive when testifying.

I spent more than twenty years as a testifying expert with Bates and its predecessor corporate entities. During that time, I testified well over 200 times in federal and state courts, U.S. Federal Bankruptcy Courts the NASD/FINRA arbitration forums, the Pacific Stock Exchange, the New York Stock Exchange, the American Stock Exchange, the National Futures Association, the Chicago Board Options Exchange, the United States Congress, and the Royal Courts of Justice in London, U.K. I have given numerous depositions, participated in scores of mediations, and have consulted on literally thousands of cases that never went to a hearing or trial, but acted as an advisor to counsel.

I am also an active arbitrator for FINRA and the National Futures Association, and served as an adjudicator on hundreds of disputes at the Chicago Mercantile Exchange. So, I have seen the process from many sides of the table. My advice and tips that follow comes from an amalgamation of experience from all angles, and much of it is common sense—but now it is all in one place.

Because of my background as a securities and derivatives lawyer (governmental, regulatory, in-house counsel, and law firm) and the co-owner and operator of a brokerage firm licensed by both the SEC and the CFTC, I was able to slip somewhat easily into the role of a consulting and testifying expert—not only as a witness, but also as a confidant of scores of excellent counsels across the United States and the U.K. For the average practitioner, the road will be a bit more difficult, but hard work and a bit a polish will go a long way.

• • •

**A Personal Aside:** *Ironically, all that professional experience became secondary to the one year (and two summers) I spent as a social studies teacher at Brittany Junior High School in University City, Missouri, in 1969-70. It was there that I learned how to relate to an audience (although junior high schoolers are less of an audience than a hormonally-fueled throng). But I somehow managed to relate to those adolescents of varying degrees of maturity, and successfully imparted at least a little knowledge of the subject matter that I understood well.*

And that is exactly what any expert needs to do: teach; impart knowledge; relate to the audience; understand the material; be convincing. It later occurred to me that **everything I learned regarding being an effective expert, I learned at Brittany Junior High School!**

It may not be as easy for a former industry professional, no matter how proficient, to gain the necessary skills and expertise, hence the aid of this book. Counsel will value your industry experience, but will also be looking for the skills you bring to the table to bring the case to a successful conclusion.

The purpose of these materials is to use my background to guide the prospective expert from "subject matter expert" to "expert witness." As indicated, the two concepts are certainly related, but not identical. The goal is to help one become that invaluable asset upon which counsel and the client relies, and to feel comfortable and proficient in every aspect of the expert witness process. That process is more than the giving of testimony (although that is certainly a critical component), but it is also, in no particular order, how you:

- Acquire the assignment
- Interact with counsel
- Prepare an effective C.V.
- Write a federal expert report
- Prepare for and give an effective deposition
- Effectively use demonstrative and evidentiary exhibits
- Relate who he/she is and why he/she is well-qualified
- Identify relevant issues and strike irrelevant issues
- Form opinions based on the facts and issues presented
- Prepare for testimony
- Survive "voir dire" and turn it into an advantage
- Give effective direct examination
- Relate to the trier of fact in a specific, meaning-ful way
- Handle the mechanics of being an expert
- Rebut the opposing expert in a methodical, effec-tive manner
- Act, carry oneself, present oneself with confi-dence in a stressful situation
- Get familiar with the litigation setting
- Listen, listen, listen

- And globally, become an integral part of the professional team to assure, to the extent possible, a
successful outcome for the client.

* * *

**Note:** *While the focus is on expert testimony, most of the areas are transferrable to that of the consulting, as opposed to the testifying, expert. While in one regard, the stress on a consulting expert is arguably less than that of a testifying expert, the necessity to "get it right" is identical.*

**Critical Note:** *Two threshold questions must be addressed before the specifics of the profession are studied and learned. Being an expert witness subjects oneself to an extremely confrontational situation; it is adversarial far beyond that which most of us have ever experienced. At times, it is not pleasant; there are many times when opposing counsel feels that it is his or her responsibility to berate, to impose ad hominem arguments, to tear down your work product; to be nasty, rude and condescending in a manner that would be unacceptable in almost any other forum or in our day-to-day interactions. It is astonishing how a panel chair, or even a judge, would allow behavior which, under any other circumstance, would be considered grossly unacceptable. Of course, not every exchange is horrific, but neither is it uncommon, and a new expert must be prepared to be spoken to as if he or she were not a professional but an object of derision. The two questions to the reader are:* **"Are you capable of withstanding this type of treatment?"** *and* **"Do you want to subject yourself to this behavior as a matter of routine?"**

*I am not, by nature, a very confrontational individual. I would prefer to work out any differences in a civilized manner. Therefore, it was quite a shock when first confronted with opposing counsel who sneered at my qualifications and scorned at my work product. Even knowing that it was all part of a process, an intricate game, did not make it any easier. The process begins with voir dire and continues through cross-examination. You will be grilled on nuances which could, under other circumstances, be nonsense. You will be asked to defend your proclivity to aid one side of the table or another. Every facet of your career will be examined not with admiration, but with scorn: "How did that position qualify you to become an expert in this matter?" "So, you are not really an expert at all, correct?"*

*Being successful in this business includes the ability and the willingness to take the harassment in stride. To be honest, not everyone can withstand the abuse—I have seen many examples of new experts being unable to cope with the abuse. It helps to understand that the treatment you will receive is just a portion of the drama which, unfortunately, is standard twenty-first century litigation practice in the United States. Think hard about entering such an adversarial field; I am proof that a non-adversarial type can succeed, and you can as well, but do understand that there are easier—and less stressful—paths to a second career.*

If you choose to continue, and I certainly hope that you do, understand that becoming an effective expert is more than the sum of the mechanics outlined here. It is a twofold, inter-related dichotomy: first, to carefully and methodically teach the trier of facts what they need to know in order to understand your point of view (and hopefully adopt that point of view) and second, to develop a relationship with everyone in the room—the triers of fact, your own counsel, the court reporter, other witnesses, and believe it or not, importantly, opposing counsel.

The effective expert links the teaching aspect with the relationships formed so that the triers of fact carefully consider every spoken word. To gain the respect of everyone in the room so that one's words are given full credence, it is essential to be:

- absolutely independent
- confident
- knowledgeable
- clear and organized
- a master of cross-examination
- understanding of your audience
- polite and non-confrontational
- a good listener
- humble
- candid
- a touch pedantic
- semi-lawyerly

**These are the characteristics of a successful expert in the financial services industry.**

Let us explore them in some depth.

# CHAPTER TWO

# CHARACTERISTICS OF A SUCCESSFUL EXPERT

Taking the characteristics one by one—and m*an*y will be expanded upon later in this book:

## 1 Be Fiercely Independent

There is nothing more important as you embark upon a career as an expert than to be independent of your counsel and your client. You have been hired as a neutral expert in the field to give opinions based upon your experience in the industry that cannot be tainted by the fact that you are being paid by one side of the table. You must always battle the temptation to "join the team" and indeed it is a fine line to walk: you and counsel prepare your testimony together; you and counsel agree on the opinions that you will proffer; you and counsel will sit together and take breaks together; you will have interviewed your major witnesses while being unable to interview the opposing witnesses; you are indeed being paid by the client who is sitting right next to you. How then do you maintain that independence as an expert?

The confusion stems from the difference between a neutral and an independent. I can be independent but not necessarily be neutral. I can have strong opinions that favor the side who pays me, but if my values and my opinions and my standards are not compromised, I can remain independent while not being neutral in the case that I present.

But giving ground on being a neutral does not mean that you are an advocate. You must guard against crossing the advocacy line. It is not an easy line to straddle. I have seen too many experts, far too many experts, become shills for their clients, casting off any semblance of independence while they try to defend the indefensible, contorting themselves into positions that have no favorable outcome. They will make statements that are easily contradicted either from earlier testimony in the same matter, or, thanks to the easy availability of transcripts, testimony from previous litigations. Their opinions simply reflect counsel's view of the case, and the experts' independence is nowhere to be found.

These experts gain a reputation as puppets; they will say anything that counsel asks them to say, and use the flimsiest evidence to justify their opinions. Their reputations precede them. They tend to move from offense to defense without anchored principles. The task of cross-examination is simplified because so much contradictory material is to be gleaned from both the internet and within the network of attorneys who are willing to share information.

The most common item of shared information is a transcript from an expert's prior testimony, including deposition testimony. Opposing counsel is delighted to have previous transcripts because your words are memorialized in opinions that may (or may not) be relevant to the facts of the instant case.

Opposing counsel is not looking for nuance, but for a way to make you appear to be offering contradicting opinions. Your previous testimony is a goldmine for finding nuggets that can be thrown at you. Be prepared; try to review, or at least recall, your own prior testimonies, and then put yourself in the shoes of opposing counsel and see what contradictions might, on the surface, pop up—then rebut them. If you know that transcripts of your previous testimonies are to be had, and you can obtain copies of those transcripts, spend a great deal of time reviewing them. It is worth your while to be prepared to show to the triers of fact the differentiating facts and factors that make it clear your opinions really do not conflict.

* * *

*Cautionary Note:* Of course, you should never be put in a situation wherein you are indeed contradicting yourself, i.e., where you are asked to become a puppet. If it looks like that is what is expected of you, I suggest you closely examine your moral footprint and make the right decision. Likewise, never let the temptation of a lucrative assignment obscure that vision of your moral footprint—the onus then is upon you to be both honorable and effective.

Unmasking the "puppet expert" is quite a sad situation; most panels and judges easily see the contradictions, and I suspect even juries do as well. The process, called "impeachment," will be quite brutal as phrase upon phrase, paragraph upon paragraph is read into the record as one tries to explain the apparent inconsistencies. If the inconsistencies are, in fact, without resolution, the compromised expert feels alone and without moral or practical reinforcement to justify the opinions that are, to everyone in the room, so obviously contrived. His or her day is finished early, as his or her opinions are disregarded and the client has quite literally paid for the damage done to the case.

Yes, an expert can do tremendous damage to a case by leaving independence at the courthouse door. It is often said that an expert cannot win a case, but can always lose one. I absolutely do not agree with the first clause, but have seen the truth in the second clause in far too many instances.

• • •

**Note:** *Arbitrations are supposed to be private dispute resolution forums which means, theoretically, that transcripts should not be available for future distribution. In fact, many transcripts emanating from arbitrations are watermarked with words such as: "Confidential; To Be Used in XYZ Arbitration Only." Well, yes and no; mostly no. In my many arbitrations, I have yet to see a transcript, offered for the purpose of impeaching an expert witness, be denied its use because somehow counsel got a copy of that forbidden fruit.*

*Court cases, of course, are public and the transcripts from those proceedings are fair game without challenge.*

**A Personal Aside:** *I was occasionally asked for transcripts of the many opposing experts against whom I have testified. I did keep some transcripts, and gave them to counsel upon such a request. Conversely, opposing counsel would often ask, through my counsel, for copies of all my own transcripts. As a hard and fast rule, I would decline because I kept none of my own transcripts for what I considered a very good reason: If I kept none, there was nothing to turn over. Obviously, it did hamper my precise recollection of my previous words, but the tradeoff of not supplying needless ammunition to opposing counsel always seemed worth it.*

*You are thus faced with two choices: The first is keeping and turning over copies of your transcripts and thus being better prepared for cross-examination by studying your own words but knowing that you have armed your opponent. The second is not keeping and therefore not turning over transcripts, but perhaps being not as well prepared—being aware that opposing counsel may have access to your words from another source. I preferred the latter, but you may prefer the former.*

Can you be a recognized expert for either side of the table, i.e., can you create a reputation for being so independent that you are the go-to expert for both claimants (or plaintiffs) and respondents (defendants)? Although it is theoretically possible and even admirable, the reality is that one does invariably develop a reputation for being a "plaintiff's expert" or a "defense expert." As hard as one might try, and as praiseworthy as it might be, it is difficult to maintain continuing detachment when dealing with hotly contested cases where your opinions are so well-known and end up being attached to one side or the other. Your opinions get attached largely because you will work with, and be called time and again, by the same attorneys who work with only one side, either claimant or respondent, and since their allegiances do not vary, yours tend to follow.

There is another reason that being an expert for both claimant and respondent is difficult: conflicts of interest. Although often asked, I would decline to testify against the large Wall Street firms of which my firm had continuing assignments. There were simply too many conflicts with ongoing research projects, professional secrets, knowledge of internal processes, personal relationships, and on and on and on. From a more practical perspective, the firms were very wary (nay, apoplectic) of allowing an expert to testify against them and then continue a relationship into the future—no matter how proficient one was. Therefore, I did take assignments against "the industry," but only if there were no recent or ongoing assignments, the firm was not a major Wall Street firm, and I was truly convinced that there was significant wrongdoing by the firm.

Having said that, it is critical, if only for purposes of *voir dire*, to try to have on your C.V. a history of assignments reflecting the side that is not your go-to preference. If you can point out to opposing counsel, and therefore the triers of fact, that X percent of your assignments were for "the other side," you are in a better position to defend against being a one-sided expert.

• • •

**Note:** *It is part of both counsels' standard repertoire, on voir dire, to try to paint an expert as working for only "one side of the table" and therefore, someone who should not be trusted as having unbiased expertise. That is, of course, largely a fiction, since most experts do fall on one side or the other, and it does not (necessarily) compromise one's integrity. It is really quite the opposite: the danger of accepting most any litigation that is offered is to become a "puppet expert" without any integrity, as detailed above. Nevertheless, there will invariably be a lengthy questioning as to why one seems to prefer one side or the other. That is one reason that I mixed in claimant (plaintiff) assignments where there were no conflicts, and I was truly offended by the alleged conduct of a broker-dealer or futures commission merchant or their representatives.*

Recognize that your own counsel has a strong incentive to try to pull you completely into his or her orbit; he or she wants to win the case, and you are a critical component on the road to a win. But to maintain your integrity, there must be a certain separation and a mutual respect for each other's views.

**Therefore, it is important to do the following:**

1.  Develop your opinions independent of counsel's input. You will have all the necessary facts available, so it is a matter of creating opinions from those facts. It's fine to discuss opinions with counsel after forming them, but to assure your integrity, it's more comfortable to have a draft outline of the opinions prepared for review of counsel rather than preparing those opinions after counsel has outlined them for you.

2.  Resist the temptation to conform to counsel's wish list. In other words, do not be pushed into any opinion in which you are not completely comfortable. Know how to say "no" or at least develop an alternative with which you are comfortable. Remember, you will be cross examined on every word of your written or oral opinion. Every word. If you do not believe exactly and entirely in what you put forth, do not present it.

3.  Assure that the opinions that you offer are completely in accord with the evidence of the case. Match your opinions against both the exhibits to be used by the other parties and your own exhibits. Look critically for discrepancies where there might be an opening for cross-examination to make critical points. This will assure that you are consistent in your opinions; i.e.,

that you believe that they conform to the evidence and not to a hope and a prayer.

4. Consider putting some physical space between you and counsel's team. It is excellent optics not to be seen eating every meal with them, not huddling with them on breaks, not coming and going together. Although arbitration panels have, in recent years, come to see and expect experts to be part of counsel's team, the appearance of independence as well as the actual independence of the expert is a valuable trait.

5. Review any of your prior opinions that might be similar to the ones being offered in the subject litigation. Make sure they are consistent and if they are not, see whether you can distinguish them from each other based on the fact patterns that might differ in significant ways. If you cannot, you have an intellectual issue, perhaps an ethical issue, that must be rectified. Remember that any discrepancies between similar opinions offered at different litigations will absolutely be the subject of cross-examination. Be prepared for this long before you take the witness stand by anticipating queries from opposing counsel.

   You should be familiar enough with your prior opinions and testimony to be able to play cross-examiner with yourself long before the hearing or trial, and verbalizing the critical factual distinctions between the various cases. **No two cases are exactly alike, and the key to not being inconsistent is to make known, if possible, those critical distinctions.** Lawyers do that constantly when taking a fact pattern and distinguishing one case that appears to be adverse from another that is more favorable. That is the heart of the legal brief, and the same principle applies to your testimony.

6.  Understand that your longevity in this field will largely depend on your reputation, and your reputation is dependent on your integrity. Your counsel will never **overtly** ask you to compromise your integrity, but sometimes the demands of litigation will cause unintended pressures to surface. Resist them.

Therefore, always remember and take to heart **ESSENTIAL RULE NUMBER ONE: Never lose sight of your integrity; maintain your independence.** It's the right thing to do both ethically and professionally.

● ● ●

**A Personal Aside:** *We can learn a great deal from the British system and how its courts treat experts. Experts are not only independent, but also required to be completely neutral, hired (but not paid)* **by the court.** *The duty of an expert is* **solely** *to the court, not to the party that engages him or her and the expert is required to sign an oath to that effect. The expert report must contain not a single hint of bias, and the enforcement of the neutrality requirement even extends to the seating arrangements in court: experts are not allowed to sit with counsel's team or his or her client. Experts must sit either by themselves or, preferably, be seated with the opposing expert.*

## 2 Be Confident

Your demeanor is critical; you are in court or in arbitration to impart knowledge, to teach, to assist the triers of fact to understand what happened and the consequences of actions taken. Everything you do must radiate confidence, which means how you dress, how you sit, how you affirm your oath to be truthful, the tone of your speech, the way you respond, i.e., solemn or lighthearted, the forcefulness of your answers.

Confidence comes with knowing that you know more than anyone else in the room regarding your testimony and that you are in the room to teach—to impart your knowledge to the triers of fact. If you can surround yourself with the nuances of testimony, the teaching becomes so much easier.

Formality is something of a dying art, but in the litigation setting, for you, the expert witness, it is mandatory. Even if the chairperson of an arbitration panel invites all participants in the room to remove their coats, if I am about to testify, my coat stays on. I always wear a suit, not a sport coat. My colors are muted. I am conscious of the way I am sitting: back straight, posture erect; It is amazing how often I hear negative comments about a witness's posture and therefore the impression that he or she is offering. You should be aware of the tone and volume of your speech—not too loud, not too soft; practice the art of enunciation and speak clearly. Nothing is more irritating to a panel, a judge, or a jury than a witness who can be heard, but not understood.

Finally, always think and pause before you speak. Most counsel will use this tip in pre-testimonial preparation with their fact witnesses; "pause then speak" does nothing to diminish your confidence, and It serves two purposes. First, it gives you time, even if it is a second or two, to make sure you understand the question. Second, it gives you the time to formulate an articulate answer to the question. We all stumble somewhat with the spoken word, but in the litigation situation, it is vital to build in a pause before answering a question, on both direct and cross, to put an order, meaning, and pattern into our answers. The pause can be very short, hardly noticeable, or if necessary and helpful, it can be longer. Remember, although your live audience may (or may not) discern it, it will never show up on a transcript.

Can your confidence move toward lightheartedness? Yes, occasionally, at certain times, but very carefully. You must have the ability to read the room, and to be absolutely confident that a joke, a laugh, or even a smile will be appropriate. Unless and until you are sure that levity would be welcome, and it will vary from situation to situation, it is far better to refrain.

But that does not mean that your personality should not shine through. It should; you will be far more effective if it does. You are not a robot; your confidence should enable you to let that judge or jury see who you are by responding to questions with varying degrees of tonality, pace, warmth, and sometimes even a bit of humor.

You will become known as a great expert if counsel remembers your testimony not only for the substance, but also for the style. Style is something that comes from experience, but keep in mind these simple tips, and tell the story in a most engaging manner. Style is also integrated with effectiveness. If you develop a storytelling style on direct examination, you will keep your audience. If you develop a style that is disarming to an aggressive cross-examiner, you are well on the way to becoming an effective expert. If your style invites participation from a judge or an arbitration panel, you can be assured that you have been absolutely effective because you have engaged those triers of fact, and engagement leads to credibility.

However, remember **Essential Rule Number Two: Confidence never, ever, invites sarcasm or condescension.** Far too many times have I seen and heard experts get annoyed at what they perceive to be an ignorant or annoying question, and their answers clearly show contempt. That can be a "kiss of death" for the client's case. That expert may (or may not) live another day, but his or her reputation will surely suffer, and those professional days may be numbered.

•   •   •

**A Personal Aside:** *A lawyer examined his own expert who clearly showed contempt for the panel, for the respondents, for respondent's counsel and for me, the opposing expert. Every question and every aside was designed to encourage disdain and outrage. It was clear that the panel was disgusted; everyone on one side of the room could see it, and yet counsel and expert motored on, insulting the panel at every turn, and predictably, suffered in the end. How that was even possible with professional counsel in a high-stakes forum was astonishing; I had never seen a more blatant display of discourtesy and self-destruction in my life.*

If you get a question from the bench or the panel that is a bit strange, nay, weird or even ignorant, go with it with grace. Answer it as if it came from Professor Einstein himself. Pretend the question was brilliant. It is an opportunity. While acknowledging the question with a welcoming demeanor, move the simplistic misunderstanding into a point you obviously need to remake. There really are no bad questions from a judge or an arbitrator; basic or fundamental questions are tremendous opportunities for you to state your opinions and your interpretations again and again.

Opposing counsel will hate the fact that you are having a dialogue with the judge or an arbitrator; your counsel will be pleased. You just need to keep educating, and those questions will certainly give you a clue as to how well or poorly the arbitrator or judge is following the facts or the arguments. Thereafter, you can adjust your subsequent testimony accordingly.

Following any judge or arbitrator question, I like to get assurance that the concern is satisfied. Rather than being condescending or nasty (I have seen plenty of both), I would politely ask if I have answered the question satisfactorily. (By putting the burden on me, i.e., "Have **I** answered your question?" rather than: "Do you now understand?" it shifts the responsibility of communication to you, the expert, removing some of the tension in the room.)

If the unusual question emanated from opposing counsel on your cross-examination, be gracious and use it as an opportunity to make your points again, and again, and again. It is an amazing opportunity; use it. Experienced counsel rarely will offer the opportunity to jump on a bad question, but if it does occur, be prepared to take full advantage of it.

And it goes without saying that you and your own counsel must never team up to disparage the triers of fact or personalize an argument against the other side of the table. That will simply backfire; do not even think of going there.

*       *       *

**Another Personal Aside:** *In the fourth week of a complicated New York arbitration regarding naked put and call options, a panelist asked me for an explanation as to what was a naked call.* **It was the fourth week;** *we had been discussing naked* *calls for a month! Undaunted, very politely, I very carefully went through the explanation, feeling that we all had somehow failed badly in our communication and "reading of the panel" skills.*

**Another Personal Aside (Sorry):** *There is no greater compliment than, after a hearing or trial concludes, for opposing counsel to ask for your business card. You will know that your presentation was stellar, your confidence was on target, if counsel implies that he would like you to join his team at some point in the future.*

## 3 Be Knowledgeable, Prepared and Well-Presented

Even though you know your subject matter better than anyone else in the room, you must convey it well through your testimony. That technique takes time, preparation, and thought. Your knowledge is second nature to you, but it is meaningless unless and until you impart that knowledge in a thoughtful, well-prepared and well-presented manner. Your reputation does not proceed you; you must earn your reputation every time you raise your hand to be sworn in.

How well-prepared must you be? It is almost axiomatic that you cannot over-prepare for a testimonial engagement. You must be confident that there is not a single sheet of paper that you cannot identify, and speak to its origins, its meanings, and the relationship between it and the issues being presented. In practical terms, that means that you will be spending untold hours going through boxes and boxes of documents (or data files), reading deposition after deposition, and studying those documents that counsel has identified as "key" to the litigation—and those that he or she has not so identified.

You will know each of those documents so well that you will never be surprised when opposing counsel puts a document in front of you and begins asking for the meaning behind that document. As soon as you see that document, your mind should be clicking off the relevance and answering the following questions:

- Who prepared it?

- What was it meant to show?

- Is it consistent with or a deviation from other documents?

- Is it controversial and, if so, why?

- Do you have a good explanation for any problematic issues that it might point to?

- Are there other copies that are slightly different, indicating various iterations at different points in time?

- Does it conform to or deviate from industry or firm standards?

In other words, you can combine your knowledge with your preparation. Your industry experience has given you the baseline from which every aspect of this case, every fact, every piece of paper, every deposition, can be filtered. No one else in the room has the capability to do exactly what you can do.

You will be able to weave excerpts of deposition testimony into your recitation of facts because you know the testimony that every witness has previously given. You might even be able to point out to counsel any discrepancy between deposition testimony and live testimony—a very helpful contribution.

You will know your own deposition perfectly; every line, every word. If you have given a deposition, it will be a very precise roadmap for opposing counsel, and it is imperative that you know **exactly** what you said in the deposition so that there are no scenes in the trial which include the following exchanges:

> "Do you recall giving a deposition on [date]?" "And in that deposition, do you recall that you stated the following. ..." "And today, you testified to the following. ...." "So, were you misinformed then or are you misinformed now?" (I use the term "misinformed" to be gentler than the stereotypical "Are you lying then, or are you lying now?")

You will be so well-informed, that if you do get into the above exchange, you can tell counsel that he or she is mistaken, and can point to a more relevant section of your deposition that explains and clears up the discrepancy.

You may also want to consider talking to any witnesses on your side's witness list who may shed some light on your opinions. It must be done with care, almost always with counsel present, certainly with counsel's permission. You legitimately want to round out your information, but you do not want to be asked on cross-examination for a detailed history of your conversations with another witness. Remember, there is no privilege in your conversations, so have a deep discussion with counsel for the necessity and propriety of interviewing witnesses. There is a fine balance: On the one hand, it is an excellent way to fulfill your duty to obtain as much information as possible before creating your expert opinions, but there is a downside in having to reveal the details of those conversations on cross-examination.

In the good old days, one had to rely on notes and a great memory to accomplish this extraordinary preparation. Now, computerized aids such as CaseMap are terrific tools to organize both the material and your thoughts. Take advantage of these tools.

* * *

**Note:** *Being incredibly well-prepared, pouring over hundreds or thousands of documents, reading the depositions of the night watchman and her cousin take time, and therefore, money. Count on counsel, or more likely, the client, to be quite sensitive to money outflows. So, be cognizant that there is an inherent tension in being perfectly prepared by spending countless hours reading before the fire and keeping the costs under control. The solution, as usual, is communication. Always tell counsel what you are doing, both at the beginning of the assignment and throughout the engagement; send invoices regularly; if you have any question as to what your assignment is or should be, ask. Surprises in the billing arena are not a good thing and will not lead to reward.*

How do you go about preparing a **well-presented** direct testimony? The key is to work with counsel in preparing an outline of your testimony and your opinions. (The next chapter explains why). Who does what preparation, and to what extent you participate in the creation and drafting of testimony must be worked out between you and counsel. But, as is discussed below, your testimony must be clear and organized. Even prior to putting pen to paper (or booting up your computer) you and counsel must be on the same page as to what the scope, the depth, and objectives of your testimony are to be.

In theory, preferably, you will work with counsel, preferably for a significant number of hours beginning many weeks prior to testimony, but the reality may be different: This is litigation, a journey like no other, and counsel will be extraordinarily engaged in preparing fact witnesses for testimony. You, as an expert, are far down on the priority list several weeks out from a trial or hearing date. Ignoring you for the time being may be a great show of confidence in your abilities, or it may simply be your order in the chronology of witnesses (let us assume it is the former). But there are two things that can be done for the sake of your sanity, confidence, and effectiveness:

First, try to get the attention of one of counsel's associates. He or she **may** be less frantic and might have the time to spend with you—to motivate and, you hope, to direct you and work with you on the areas that need attention. That work will pay enormous benefits once lead counsel pivots to your testimony and the specific needs of the client.

Second, try writing your own testimony. Be aware, however, that this is an advanced skill that comes after many forays into the lion's den. Some very good experts never write their own testimony. But if you are so inclined, once you have gained confidence, preparing your own direct testimony is an enormous assistance to counsel and a significant help to you in better understanding the case and where you can be of assistance. It relieves counsel of an immense task at a critical time in the hearing or trial—immediately before closing arguments, assuming you are on defense. You can do this only, assuming, again, relevant experience as a condition-precedent, and if the issues and facts are well known and understood, and that you are exactly on point with what counsel needs from you.

I always start my own testimony as an outline, but it usually morphs into a question format, and from there, it morphs further into a question format with detailed self-suggested answers. Come testimony time, I never try to memorize the answers (they are there for counsel to use as a checklist and for prompting purposes), but I do internalize the gist of the proposed answer.

However, I will **always** memorize items contained in a list of items. Why? A list is one of those things that screams "write me down." And if it says, "write me down" then the trier of fact will, with a little informal prompting, do exactly that. And a list will allow me to address any issue that contains components in depth, with organization, and clarity.

For example, I used to tell panels that there were always five, and only five, duties that a non-discretionary securities broker owed to his or her client. Then I would list them, using the "R" at the beginning of each duty as a memory device for: rapid execution; receiving authorization; recommending only suitable securities; not misrepresenting; and refraining from self-dealing. Having been prompted that what follows is a list of five items, the panel or jury would write them down, and I would then return to the top of the list, and go into depth vis à vis the facts of the case.

By the way, the list was bulletproof because it was grounded in an extensive line of often-affirmed court cases, so that when opposing counsel objected to "legal testimony," I was prepared to defend the list not only with the cases, but with the observation that it had now become uncontroverted. I also involved my counsel before I delved into this line of testimony so that he or she could effectively argue any objection that opposing counsel might interject.

• • •

**A Personal Aside:** *When I'm working with counsel who trusts me and I'm confident that my testimony is well-done and on point, there is no greater compliment and feeling of accomplishment than to have counsel take my outline or questions and answers the night before the trial or hearing, and simply use it, intact, the following day without any meaningful prep. I always hold my breath, hoping that counsel has read and understood it, but when working with accomplished counsel, that has never been a problem.*

Finally, well-organized, well-prepared and well-presented testimony must never be generic testimony. Testifying only to a class of issues rather than the fact-specific issues of a particular litigation can be detrimental or even fatal to your client's case. It screams to a judge, jury or arbitration panel that you are either lazy and you have not taken the time to prepare for your testimony, or that your normal methodology is to give standardized academic lectures which, while perhaps interesting, have limited usefulness to triers of fact who need context in expert testimony.

• • •

**Another Personal Aside:** *A well-known expert is indeed knowledgeable by any measure, testifies constantly—perhaps more than anyone else in the field, but because of the frequency of the testimony, that expert refuses to take the time to be fact-specific, only testifying to theory behind the issues. The expert freely admits to never having interviewed* *the client, not knowing the specific factual nuances of the litigation, and therefore severely limits the effectiveness of the testimony. This leaves the door wide open for brutally effective cross-examination on the specific facts that may moot much, or all, of the testimony, e.g., "If you had known X, would that have changed your opinion?" "If you had known Y, would that have changed your opinion?" "Did you hear Z testify which directly contradicts your assumptions?"*

It further gives you, if you are a defense expert testifying last in sequence, the opportunity to dismantle the testimony of the opposing expert by putting the opinions in specific context of the litigation at hand. When testifying against this specific expert, I would always move from the generic lecture on the "horrible product" or the "fraud on the public" to detailed defenses based not just on the data, but the testimony of those who bought the product, sold the product, and/or supervised the transaction. I would examine the pattern of trading and explain the statistics, not in a vacuum, but in relation to the facts of the case. Getting specific is far more effective than giving a generic lecture on product type or data.

# 4 Be Clear—Be Organized

The heart of expert testimony are the opinions offered. You are on the witness stand to give your opinions; you hold a unique position within the scope and hierarchy of the cast of characters being introduced to the triers of fact. All **fact** witnesses will be admonished to stick only to what they know first-hand, and should not, absolutely must not, give opinions within their testimony. Experts, on the other hand, are not only allowed to give opinions, but are expected to do so. You are specifically allowed to offer "opinion testimony" on all issues before the panel or the court, including the ultimate issue before the panel or the court.

Special sections are carved out within the procedural rules of FINRA, and state and federal courts that relate solely to expert testimony. I have detailed some of the federal rules in Chapter Five, namely Federal Rules of Evidence 702 and Federal Rules of Civil Procedure 26. The FINRA Rule applicable to expert witnesses is procedural, found in Rule 12602: "Absent persuasive reasons to the contrary, expert witnesses should be permitted to attend all hearings." In addition, in describing the arbitration process to prospective claimants, FINRA, on its website, explains the role of the expert as follows: "...each claimant can ask expert witnesses who have specialized training or knowledge to testify as to their opinion on a technical matter to help the arbitrators draw conclusions and render a decision."

Go to those rules found in Chapter Five; learn them—but the point is that you, as an expert witness, do hold a unique place within the litigation scene and you must take full advantage of it by hitting the issues hard with your opinion testimony, in effect, making a summary, pre-closing argument on behalf of counsel.

* * *

**Note:** *There was, for many years, a conflict as to whether experts could offer testimony on the "ultimate issue;" e.g., was the firm in violation of rules, regulations, customs and practices in the industry. Through recent court decisions, and then rule changes, that barrier has been effectively removed,* *although in the arbitration process, it was usually allowed anyway. However, it may be that counsel does not want you to testify on the "ultimate issue." Perhaps there are multiple experts, or perhaps counsel wants to save that for his or her closing arguments. It is a point to be discussed with counsel when forming opinions to be presented.*

Most often, because our brains crave patterns and organization, I will preview all my opinions sequentially at the outset of my testimony, and then dive back into them one by one. All triers of fact appreciate the organization of this type of testimony, will take numbered notes and will, therefore, receive the testimony far, far better than a disjointed presentation. I call this the "pencil test" because it gives the triers of fact the opportunity to take pencil (i.e., pen) in hand and be guided through my opinions sequentially. I look at my proposed order of testimony and ask myself: "Does this pass the "pencil test?" As a corollary, whenever possible and for the same reasons, I do make points with deliberate numeric sequences, e.g., "Let me answer that in three parts: First…"

Remember, listeners give various weights to opinions depending on numerous factors, and clarity and organization are, in my experience, even more important than background and credentials which, once established, tend to fade into the woodwork.

Organizing your testimony in this manner all but insures that the judge, jury or panel will understand your testimony. They might not agree with it, but they will clearly see where you are coming from and will have an organized basis during their deliberations.

Hit the most important opinion first, e.g., "My first opinion is that there was no churning in the account because the three indicia of churning, namely control of the account, excessive trading of the account, and intent to benefit the broker rather than the client are entirely absent..." Then, after doing the same for all the proffered opinions, return to number one (and they will be numbered, right?) and dive deeper through a question from counsel such as: "Let us return to your first opinion, number one: Can you explain your reasoning for that opinion?" From there, you methodically go through the elements of churning—one by one—and relate them to the facts of the case.

*  *  *

**Note:** *You must be on the same page with your counsel; this progression and every technique and tip that is mentioned here might become part of your routine, but communication with counsel is vitally important. For example, counsel may not want you to preview your opinions; counsel may not want a sequential recitation of your qualifications. That is all well and good—but your job is to talk these things over with counsel well in advance of your testimony.*

Remember, again, you are teaching, and that has two components: First, you are giving a mini lecture on the scope of the "law" of churning (without necessarily going into the law—see below), i.e., teaching the panel what is the well-accepted definition of churning (or, obviously, any other issue), and second, you are directly relating the facts of the case at hand to that definition. The more you draw on the facts of the case at hand, and move away from solely giving a lecture on churning, the more effective the presentation will be.

What if you encounter an objection to your testimony stating that you are not qualified to tell the panel the nature or scope of the law? First, always remember that answering an objection is not your responsibility; it belongs solely with counsel; wait for counsel to respond. Say nothing. Look at the panel. Relax. Second, you should be prepared to put all such testimony in the context not of "the law," but in terms such as "it is well settled that…" or "there is broad agreement on the definition of…" or "it is the custom and practice of the industry…" I have found that using language such as that makes an objection more difficult to sustain. You may still have to explain why you believe something is "well-settled," or having "broad agreement," but in doing your homework, whether your own research or with the assistance of counsel, you should be prepared to have an answer ready if opposing counsel returns to the issue on cross-examination.

Being organized is the first key to being clear. If you and counsel have an organized presentation, your points will or should be clear to the triers of fact. But there is one more component to clarity: your exhibits.

The precious charts, graphs and tables that you worked on so hard with your staff and counsel should be clear as well. That means they must be easy to understand and further the assignment of telling your story.

At every opportunity during preparation, ask yourself, and your associates, questions such as:

- Is this clear and easy to understand?

- Can I make the same point clearer without sacrificing any important data?

- Can your average juror understand this graph and relate it to my testimonial points?

- Does this table illustrate the points that I will be making or does it add nothing to my testimony?

- Is it necessary to be shown and admitted as evidence, or can we "back-pocket" it and use it only as backup if challenged?

- Are the colors and fonts perfect; i.e., distinctive but not distracting?

- Is it unintentionally misleading?

- Does this really help my testimony or is it a distraction?

- If it does help my testimony, am I prepared to weave it seamlessly into that testimony?

- Will this graph invite controversy, and if so, is it worthwhile?

Those questions, and many more should be considered when preparing visuals for introduction as evidence.

Visuals are an extraordinary tool in a litigation setting; every eye in the room will instantly go to a projected exhibit or to a colorful graphic in an exhibit book. It breaks up the verbal testimony, introducing a new aspect to the proceedings. It gives you, the expert, a tool to extract attention, and points made while using a visual aid are more powerful than the simple spoken word. Even badly done exhibits demand attention, but badly done exhibits draw the immediate attention and the ire of the cross-examiner and will backfire emphatically. Little is more deflating, and damaging to one's case, than having to admit that a chart or graph is incorrect, improperly drawn, or is based on the wrong data. That is why they must be bulletproof. So, I would never discourage the use of visual exhibits; just make sure they are as strong and precise as your testimony.

• • •

**A Personal Aside:** *In my final testimony, I violated my own rules and failed to scrutinize a graph with the necessary detail before it was presented to an arbitration panel. Opposing counsel was merciless, even though the "error" was mechanical, not substantive, simply not completely and accurately aligning a single data point with the appropriate axis. The data and notations were correct; the placement was a bit off. The cross-examination was endless, moving from the specifics of that data point to a request that all exhibits be rejected due to the "erroneous work of the respondent's expert" and rather vicious ad hominem attacks on me and my firm. The request was denied, but there is no question that I unnecessarily opened that door. Do as I say, not…*

**Another Personal Aside:** *I was a member of The Securities Expert's Roundtable for many years, a group of experts in the financial field who would get together annually to exchange pertinent and timely ideas and experiences.*

*Several years ago, I gave a presentation that focused on the "unintentionally misleading" aspect of visual aids. (Actually, in some cases that I found, the misleading part could have been intentional—but that is for another day.) The gist of the lecture was that manipulation of data* **upon presentation** *can greatly influence the look, and therefore, the proposed conclusions to be derived from the visual.*

*For example, playing with the scale and the timeframe of a graph will always change the angle of the data presented. One can always make the slope of a line look either steeper or shallower depending on those factors. Cherry-picking time frames, even when there is a rational reason for so doing, is a perfect example of presenting data in a manner that might be considered misleading.*

*In this regard, consider a graph whose Y axis, representing a percentage, ranges from 95 to 100. Two items along the X axis are being compared. The visual difference between two items that scored 99 and 94 respectively would span almost the entire length of the graph. However, if the scale was adjusted to represent percentages between 0 and 100, the difference between the two items would appear to be visually insignificant. Be very aware!*

*I was a bit taken aback when I examined scores of my own visuals that had been accepted as evidence and saw the possibility of "unintentional misleading." This is another area where pre-trial preparation is vital to, at the very least, being prepared to answer some tough questions. Remember, counsel on the other side of the table is probably aware of this issue and will, if he or she considers it misleading, call you out on it.*

The second key to being clear is moderation in the use of industry jargon. You have probably been in the industry for most of your adult life, and you have probably lived and breathed the intricacies of the language of the industry for that same period. But those who are listening to you are neophytes regarding your strange language, and unlike a beginning Berlitz course, being able to speak "industry" scores you no points. Once qualified as an expert, it is understood that you know the language, but if your job is to educate—and it is—then the use of industry jargon is simply distracting from your presentation.

It is far better to use familiar words, even at the expense

of appearing to simplify your testimony, then to try to dazzle your listeners with "insider-speak." It is a conscious choice that you might have to practice. For example, instead of saying "FINRA," you might want to say, "the industry regulator," instead of saying "FOCUS Report," say "the required financial report."

Take a tip from moderators on television news talk shows. Whenever a panelist blurts out an acronym or a piece of "insider-speak," he or she is immediately inter-rupted by the moderator with an explanation of what was just said. Be your own moderator, and if you find yourself having said something that may not be well-understood, pause, give the common word explanation, and move on. It will be well-received and appreciated.

Finally, remember to assess your audience: I never expect a jury to be able to comprehend even the most rudimentary industry jargon. I know an arbitration panel is probably more sophisticated, but I always err on the side of the use of more common-language.

# 5  Cross-Examination; a Survival Guide

When I was very new to the business of expert witnessing, I was astonished when my late friend and partner, Larry Keating, said to me, "I absolutely love cross-examination." He went on and on about how this was his moment to shine, to go toe-to-toe with the best, to use his intellect, and that cross-examination is where he goes to "win."

It astonished me for several reasons. First, it is perfectly natural to be terrified of cross-examination. I was. After all, you are about to be attacked, and so are your work product, motives, theories, knowledge, and confidence. You are dealing with a skilled litigator who has perfected the art form to which you are the target. Why not be anticipatorily terrified of cross-examination?

Second, how in the world can one shine on cross-examination? Are we not taught that the long, explanatory answers are developed on direct examination and cross-examination is reserved for the terse, tell-them-the-bare-minimum answers? And if that is so, how can you shine?

Larry was absolutely right, although it took quite a while for me to understand and internalize what he was saying. It took even longer before I became eager for cross, and looking forward to opposing counsel to rise and approach.

Understand the motive of the cross examiner: He or she is looking to find holes or contradictions in your story or your work product and discredit you so that your opinions are given little or no weight in the eyes of the triers of fact. The *ad hominem* arguments really are not personal, but a means to an end. The cross examiner is on offense and you are on defense, leading to two avenues of development.

First, if there are no discrepancies in your story or in your work product, there is nothing to exploit. That alone should give you confidence. If you are absolutely confident about your direct testimony and you are solid in your opinions and your exhibits, then opposing counsel can only nibble around the edges and, indeed, when nibbling, offer you golden opportunities for you to reinforce everything that you stated in your direct examination.

That is not to say that opposing counsel will concede that you are wonderful, articulate, an immense help to the triers of fact, and then thank you for your appearance. No, he or she will continue to press, to make misleading or provocative statements, to try to anger you, to attempt to get you to open a door that should remain shut. He or she will use every word you said on direct, every word or figure contained in an exhibit that you prepared to find where there might be that hole or that contradiction.

Opposing counsel will have had the services of his or her own expert or experts who have poured over your exhibits in advance and have given reams of notes, most of them useless. But even useless notes can give an examiner an opening to inquire. And inquire they will. Most cross-examinations are at least twice the length of a direct, since it is an exercise in probing for the soft spot. Remember, in arbitration, there is generally no allowance for deposition testimony which, if allowed, would have brought into focus the relevant areas for cross-examination. Therefore, prob-ing for the soft spot on cross-examination contains many of the elements which would have been accomplished in a deposition, and tends to lengthen the amount of time spent on your cross.

Occasionally, the opposite may occur. Opposing coun-sel, in his or her wisdom, may recognize that you are skilled, that there is little to be gained from incessant probing, and that, in fact, there might be clear and present danger in doing so. Knowing this, he or she will conduct only a cursory examination: perhaps a foray into your credentials, perhaps an innocent question about an exhibit, perhaps a question or two about the source of an opinion—and that might be it. That usually shows good judgment, although, frankly, it often left me with a sense of disappointment.

Second, you have the opportunity to turn defense into offense. This is hard; it is a learned procedure; it is going to be awkward at first; but it is the art of knowing when to strike. If keeping the answers short is an Essential Rule (see below), knowing when to strike, to turn defense into offense, is just as essential.

If counsel gives you the opportunity to expand upon a critical issue, one that is still in contention, grab it. If the question opens the door for a fusillade from you that reiterates the points you made on direct, run with it. It might be an unartfully phrased question such as: "So your opinion was that my client had a duty to complain, isn't that so?" Answer clearly: "No, that is not what I said. My opinion was…" Go through your reasoning again; explain to the panel or the jury again what your opinion was and why. Do it in depth. Very seldom will a judge or an arbitration chair cut you off when counsel has opened the door for you to do a full explanation. That is what you are doing: explaining, teaching, using the forum to your advantage after finding an opening.

I have come to understand that cross-examination is very much like a boxing match. Understand, though, that for a while, you are not in the heavyweight division, but your examiner probably is. Therefore, until you get the hang of it, perhaps rope-a-dope (with a tip of the hat to Ali) is in order. But after a few bouts, you can learn to stay off the ropes, circle, jab, play defense, and then when you see an opening, go for it. The ring is yours, and you can score point after point. (But please don't expect a knockout; you're not that good—yet).

Cross-examination is where your opinions will be crystalized in the minds of the triers of fact. Everyone in the room knows that your direct testimony, like any direct testimony, is somewhat scripted. You and counsel worked hard on a way to tell your story, to advance your opinions in the best possible manner. But on cross, you have no script; it is you and your cross examiner parrying back and forth. It is the boxing match. If you hold firm to your opinions, and they stand the test of cross-examination, then those opinions become solidified with the judge, jury, or arbitration panel. Your counsel can then easily and gladly weave your testimony into the closing argument. That is why cross is so exhilarating.

But get back to basics: the first rule of cross-examination might seem contradictory to the enthusiasm I have just explained. That rule is this: In general, keep your answers short and simple. In fact, let's call it **ESSENTIAL RULE NUMBER THREE: On cross-examination, keep your answers short and simple.**

The object is to make opposing counsel work, dig deeper and not be handed a gift. If you keep your answers short, you do not open avenues that are not yet explored; you force counsel to do the difficult work of finding any chinks in your armor while you simply await the next exploratory question.

You are in control of the cross-examination. Hard to believe, but true. Simple yes/no answers are fine if they do not require elaboration. But if they do, answer yes/no, but then go forward with more information. If counsel demands only a yes or no answer, he/she may try to force you into a situation denying you the opportunity for elaboration. But it is your right to be heard and to fully answer a question. Go ahead and ignore the directive to answer only "yes or no." State firmly and unequivocally that a yes/no answer is not possible without misleading the court or the panel. A plea to the bench or the chair that you are being uncooperative will be denied unless the situation is clearly meriting only a yes/no format. But that situation is rare.

So, in general, answer the question and resist the temptation to elaborate; you will have that opportunity on re-direct. But also recognize that there are situations where the opposite is true: You want to elaborate, but opposing counsel wants shorter answers. You really are in control.

* * *

**A Personal Aside:** *Testifying in federal court, I had a miscommunication with counsel. Counsel decided to do only a cursory direct examination of me with the intention of a more robust examination on re-direct. (Don't ask...) Cross was intense, loud, and full of theatrics, and I decided to quell the fire by sticking only to the very shortest, simple answers (see Essential Rule Number Three, above), believing that I could make my essential points on re-direct. That strategy infuriated my own counsel who took me aside during a break and screamed, literally screamed: "You're giving away the farm, make this the worst day of his life; fight him at every turn." So much for Essential Rule Number Three. So, my tone changed, I was no longer defensive, but took the offense at every available turn, not waiting for re-direct. Rules must be flexible; strategies must be communicated.*

**I have eighteen tips for a successful cross-examination:**

1.  You must relax. No matter how many times one undergoes the process, it is still an ordeal, and it is stressful. So, whatever tension-relieving techniques you have that work for you—employ them.

2.  Remember the earlier tips about being confident, well-organized, and well-prepared? Be confident, well-organized and well-prepared.

3.  Be non-confrontational and listen extraordinarily well.
    You must respect your examiner, do not ever show any
    hostility, either verbally or through body language,
    and listen extremely carefully to the question so that
    you do not inadvertently open any doors for counsel.
    Also, as explained in more detail below, hesitate before
    answering every question. Give yourself a moment to
    hear the question, digest the question, formulate an
    answer—before beginning to answer.

4.  Have nothing in front of you when your examina-
    tion begins. Bring nothing to the table or the witness
    box. Close any materials that might be in front of
    you. It increases your concentration and displays
    your confidence. You should be given any materials
    necessary for referral—but if not, you are entitled to
    ask for them.

5.  Address your answers to the judge, jury, or the arbi-
    tration panel. I like to look at counsel during the
    question and then immediately pivot to the judge,
    jury, or the arbitration panel—always rotating my
    attention among the various members of the jury or
    panel. Speaking directly to the triers of fact greatly
    increases your rapport and allows you to set up the
    crucial communication link to those who will make
    the ultimate decision on the issues. Questions from
    the judge or panel are more likely to flow to you (a
    very good thing) if you are speaking directly to them.
    However, counsel may have a different preference;
    respect that and adapt.

6.  In a difficult situation, never, ever, look to your coun-
    sel for help. He or she cannot help you, and it just
    looks bad; really bad. You have no alternative other

than to carry on and try to answer the question as best that you can. However, the good news is that any hesitation in answering a question should cue your counsel to think carefully about the question, why you might be hesitating, and therefore might cue counsel to either immediately pose an objection or a note-to-self to pursue the issue on your redirect examination.

7. If there is an objection to a question from your counsel, immediately stop talking. Wait for counsel to argue the point of that objection, and then wait for a ruling from the judge or the arbitration chair. For the moment, you are just a piece of furniture. Enjoy it; your ordeal will resume shortly.

8. If given a break during your cross-examination, do not approach your counsel. Keep your distance. You are expected not to converse with counsel while your cross-examination is active, and it is still considered active at a break or even overnight. Some arbitration panels relax this rule, either overtly or by not saying anything about the issue. But that really does not matter; you should respect the concept and remain detached from contact with counsel and the team. Federal courts will never relax the rule and will admonish a witness who has had contact with counsel during cross-examination. If counsel requests a debriefing in the midst of your cross-examination, explain your concerns and let it be known that you prefer not to converse. If counsel persists, I can suggest only that you now know the ground rules; proceed as you must.

9. Establish a non-verbal line of communication with your counsel during cross-examination when you

want to signal that a point needs elaboration or clarification on re-direct. A simple glance or a nod of the head should do it. That type of message is totally unlike the process of looking to counsel for assistance. Experienced counsel will immediately pick up on your signal and you can be assured that your request will be fulfilled.

10. If you feel a question is objectionable, while you cannot verbally "object," you can hesitate long enough to give your counsel a clue that he or she should consider an objection. Sometimes this works, sometimes not. Do not try to play lawyer too often; have faith in your counsel that a truly objectionable question will elicit an objection.

11. Always, in your mind and to yourself, carefully examine the premise of a cross-examination question. This is critically important. Setting forth a false or misleading premise to a question that is otherwise perfectly fine is one of the oldest lawyerly "techniques."

   For example: Question: "And after reviewing all the documentation, the committee determined the price of the IPO was to be $140, correct?" That question implied, was premised on, an assumption that all documentation was reviewed. Was it? Was it only relevant documentation? Was any critical documentation missing from a review? Is that what the litigation is all about? Be very careful and think about the premise of each question.

   Not all misleading questions are deliberate; some can occur innocently simply because financial matters are complex even to experienced attorneys. But either way, part of listening carefully to a question is to mentally check whether you agree with the premise.

If you do not, do not answer the question, but instead, ask for the question to be rephrased. If the rephrased question still does not satisfy you, state something along the lines of:

"I still am unable to answer that question because I disagree with the premise within the question. You stated 'X,' and I disagree with that, therefore I cannot in good faith answer that question."

Asking for a question to be rephrased is your absolute right. This request will always result in counsel complying, but may also give rise to a dialogue between you and counsel as to **why** you disagree with the premise of the question. That is fine; you should be fully prepared to explain and take that opportunity to drive home a point.

The use of improper premises is especially true when being cross-examined on your expert report or expert opinions. You know those opinions far better than opposing counsel. He or she is trying to dissect the opinions and/or the rationales behind the opinions. In doing so, a great number of suppositions may be given to you that are simply untrue or inapplicable. Be extremely cognizant of any incorrect premise when defending your opinions.

This tip is so important that I have called it **ESSENTIAL RULE NUMBER FOUR: Always examine the premise of a cross-examination question and never answer a question that is improperly premised.**

12. If you truly do not understand a question, do not guess as to what counsel meant. The question may be deliberately vague in the hope that you will take the bait and fill in what counsel does not know, or what he or she does know but wants to see how much you know or are willing to supply. Alternatively, the ques-

tion may be unintentionally obtuse; lawyers are not (always) perfect. Either way, you have no obligation to answer a vague or imperfect question. As stated above, it is perfectly acceptable to ask counsel to rephrase the question.

13. Be wary of hypotheticals. You are an expert witness and therefore, unlike for a fact witness, hypothetical questions are permitted. But hypotheticals must have a rational nexus to the facts presented in the litigation at hand. Your counsel will object if the hypothetical is not connected, at least tangentially, to the present reality, but if counsel does not object, you must be alert and pro-active.

   If after receiving what I consider to be an inappropriate hypothetical, I would pause, for an extended period, and ask if the question was, in fact, related to the matter at hand. I might ask, somewhat rhetorically, whether the question is hypothetical or not. That might bring a rebuke from counsel, but it also alerts both your counsel and the triers of fact, that there is a problem with the question. If directed to answer, do so, but in your answer, take the opportunity to point out the discrepancies between the hypothetical and what you consider to be the reality of the facts as developed. There may be more admonitions, but so be it. Do not be afraid to engage opposing counsel; remember that this is sparring and if you are composed and polite, it is perfectly acceptable to resist.

14. Be very aware of cadence. Cross-examiners like to get witnesses into a rhythm where it is easy to agree with the early softball questions, but then move to the more substantive questions where witnesses often find themselves in a general state of continued agreement

with counsel. Guard against this by doing two things: First, create your own rhythm; pause before answering, slow down the tempo of your responses alternating with an increased pace or tone. Second, be aware of the cadence trick and when appropriate, simply say "no" to a question, or ask for a clarification, or that the question be repeated. The unexpected answer breaks the rhythm, throws off the entire technique, and resets the examination. If you are aware of what opposing counsel is doing, you can easily defeat the strategy. But remember, more important than style is your substantive responses to the questions however phrased. Be alert and never lose sight of your mission.

15. Never, ever go out on a limb. Never guess the answer to a question. Never, ever prevaricate. Be extraordinarily careful with your words. Remember the old Road Runner cartoons where Wile E. Coyote would saw off the wrong part of the tree and just hang there in mid-air until he realized that down was the only way out? That would be you if you believe that you can outsmart your questioner because you believe that you are smarter than he or she. That would be you if you toss out a "throwaway" line that is not grounded in the facts of the case or an opinion that is not confirmed by the evidence. That line, that answer, which you so smugly, or even innocently, threw into the mix may very well be seized upon and kneaded and reworked, through repeated questioning to you, until it is central to your opponent's case—all because you really, really wanted to emphasize a point, or make yourself look better, or for whatever reason those words slipped through your lips. Instead, you are now enduring a most uncomfortable line of ques-

tioning that you brought upon yourself. There is never a reason to go out on a limb; you must be fully grounded instead.

A more innocent relative of "going out on a limb" is to "hedge an answer."

**Q:** "After hearing the evidence in this matter, do you still believe that Colonel Mustard killed Miss Scarlet in the Conservatory with the candlestick?"

**A:** "That is my expert opinion, but I now also believe that it is also possible that the Billiard Room was the scene of the murder, and I believe the evidence could support the use of a rope used by Professor Plum."

No. Your hedged answer just opened the door to a whole new line of questions and essentially destroyed your credibility. If you really do not believe your expert opinion is solid, if you believe that there is room to hedge, it should not be your expert opinion. That is part of your pretrial or prearbitration preparation. When, during that preparation, you questioned yourself on every one of your opinions, make sure that you need not hedge.

In the rare case where evidence is uncovered during the hearing or trial that causes you to change your opinion, you must think long and hard about your opinion; e.g., why any newly discovered evidence survived the discovery phase and how strong is that evidence that it might alter one of your well-researched opinions. As discussed later, there are consequences to withdrawing an opinion that has already been exchanged, but more fundamentally, you must ask yourself to weigh the alternative theories and decide which is more solid. In most cases, your expert opinion, which has been grounded in your experience and the documentary evidence that you have internalized, will be the one that will survive scrutiny. It is therefore essential that the answer to the question above is: "No. It remains my firm opinion that Colonel Mustard killed Miss Scarlet in the Conservatory with the candlestick—and again, here is why…"

16. Every word and phrase must be spoken with a purpose in mind; that is why you practice your direct examination and anticipate your cross-examination. It is not an easy lesson to learn simply because that is not how we converse our day to day lives. We are not used to thinking through every sentence for the implications of our words, because in normal conversation, there is usually no adverse consequence. However, in litigation, for the expert witness, that is simply not true. Every word is open to a follow-up question as to what was meant. Every phrase is subject to examination and re-examination.

    The learning curve here is somewhat steep. You must be aware that every one of your words has consequences, but you must also develop a style that does not appear to be stilted. If you speak with great hesitation, it might easily be interpreted as vacillation or uncertainty—in contravention of your desire to be confident and to be an influencer. Experience is truly the best teacher in this regard, but in embarking on this path, keep in mind the duality of verbal consequences and effective communication.

17. Do not guess at an answer. You may think that your response to a difficult question is an "educated guess," but no, it is still a guess and answering such a ques-

tion that way can lead to disaster. The undeniable fact is that opposing counsel undoubtedly knows the answer and is waiting for you to fall into a trap. Sure, it is an old litigation trick (technique), but it is easily avoided by asking yourself this simple question: "Do I know, absolutely know, the answer from the facts and materials at hand?" The proper response to a question that would require a guess, educated or not, is "I do not know the answer to that question and I am unwilling to venture a guess." That answer squares with the fundamental advice that counsel gives every fact witness: "Don't guess." Assuming that the question is not fundamental to your expertise or one of your expert opinions, you will never be criticized for the "I do not know..." answer. It forces the opposing counsel to move on or at least to narrow the question by reference to a specific line of testimony or a document in evidence. And by so narrowing the question, it allows you to answer the question based upon your knowledge of the facts.

Fact witnesses are always advised by counsel that "I don't know" or "I don't remember" are perfectly acceptable answers. Experts can take a cue from that advice, although hopefully, the demurs will be infrequent and definitely not in the areas of the professed expertise. Keep in mind that "I don't know" is far preferable to any type of guess.

18. It goes without saying that you must never lie, fib, misstate, or prevaricate. Why would you do so? You cannot win with that type of statement on the record. It will come back to hurt you either during the trial or arbitration or later when the record is examined by another opposing counsel. Barring pure dishonesty or stupidity, the only reason I could think of to

prevaricate is that your preparation was inadequate and now you must scramble for answers and damn the consequences. If it is your qualifications that are the subject, do not even think about misstating; the fact-checking these days is too easy and too pervasive. You will be caught, and your good reputation will be eradicated. If the subject is what you read or reviewed to form your opinions, remember that the question is just a prelude to a quiz, and you will be caught if you lie about what you reviewed. If the question concerns background on your opinions, fess up if counsel shows you materials which you might have overlooked. Be honest and truthful. Sometimes it hurts, but the alternative is much worse.

My dear friend Larry Keating was right; cross-examination can be exhilarating and opportunistic. Done right, it can cement your opinions in the eyes of the triers of fact, and it will become the most rewarding part of your career.

## 6 Understand Your Audience

There is an enormous difference between speaking to an arbitration panel whose members can be disdainful of experts and may believe that they know, if not everything, at least enough to decide long before you begin your testimony or to a judge who may be skeptical, but can be persuaded that your testimony is both relevant and meaningful, or lastly to a jury who really does know nothing about your subject matter and needs to be captured and engaged. It is critical to internalize to whom you are speaking with and adjust accordingly.

As a generalized overview, arbitration panels can be

a bit disdainful of experts; they often believe that they do not need an expert for them to decide a case—sometimes they even say so aloud. A judge, depending on his or her knowledge of the subject matter, will either be appreciative or dismissive of an expert. A jury will generally be receptive, up to a point; hearing an expert on a matter in which they are quite confused is looked upon as a lifeline. However, if it goes on too long or is too technical in nature, there is a tendency to lose a jury.

● ● ●

**A Personal Aside:** *Testifying in Cleveland, Claimant's expert was told by the panel that his services were not needed. The panel was comprised of [allegedly] experienced professionals and could decide the matter without experts on either side—which also included me. Claimant's counsel was not pleased and told the panel they interfered with his right to present his case in the way he preferred. The panel stayed firm, dismissed both experts, and proceeded without us. Upon appeal to the Ohio Supreme Court, the panel was rebuked and told to go back and hear expert testimony before rendering another verdict. Obviously, the verdict remained the same. The takeaways from that decision were that a panel cannot assume expert testimony is irrelevant to them, that counsel does indeed have a right to present his or her case as seen fit, and that there are limits to a panel's authority.*

There are no hard and fast rules on how to best prepare for your appearance before an arbitration panel. Panels on the whole vary greatly in their experience, their temperament, and their knowledge. Even within a panel, there may be striking differences in how well individual members understand the nuances of the industry. Therefore, if possible, it is wise to concentrate your efforts on educating an individual panelist on that which you believe is necessary. It will not take long to garner clues as to which member is following an argument and which ones are not. Look for clues in body language if there are no oral interruptions. If you feel that a point is being missed, carefully inquire whether you have made yourself clear. You do not want to insult anybody, but the stakes are high, and you must be willing to gently press to assure that your client is being well-served.

In general, start with the assumption that the panelists have a modicum of knowledge about the industry and try to gauge how true that is. Avoid jargon, but state your case as if your audience are professionals; they will appreciate your consideration. But be very willing, even eager, to strike a balance between a presentation to professionals and a basic tutorial on securities.

I have found that the panel chair is usually the key to understanding how well your material is being received. Look to the chair when a complex point is made. Despite being trained to be absolutely passive, he or she will usually give a non-verbal clue as to how well you have done. The chair does not necessarily speak (verbally or not) for the panel, but it is an excellent beginning point.

If you are getting clues that the panel is hostile to expert testimony (in general, not necessarily aimed at your testimony), consider trying to engage in expert-to-panel dialogue. I will often pose a question to the panel regarding the point made, subtly (or not) asking for a dialogue. I do like to break down the passivity that FINRA likes to see in its arbitrators. Nothing disarms a hostile panel like an intellectual discussion where you can prove that your expertise, and the materials that you have prepared, can indeed add to panel's understanding. Once a dialogue has begun with one panelist, it is almost inevitable that the remainder of the panel will jump in with similar or related questions. The back-and-forth is tremendously helpful on two fronts; first, to cool any animosity, and second, to advance your substantive arguments.

Again, as in so many aspects of becoming an expert witness, there is a learning curve, and good judgement must prevail.

On to a jury trial. Assume the jury knows nothing. Yes, they are perfectly wonderful people who are giving up personal and/or work hours to be paid a mighty $20 (or so) a day plus $3 a day for parking. They are probably, justifiably, a bit annoyed for having to be in court, and now they are faced with a dry financial dispute rather than a sexy murder-for-hire trial. Bummer. But as down-to-earth as these jurors are, unfortunately, your world and their world rarely intersect, at least professionally. Your job as teacher is more important than ever. You must educate without talking down to them. You must go slowly without appearing condescending. You must somehow connect with them even though you are wearing your best Brooks Brothers (or St. John's) suit and they may be wearing their finest running outfits.

But connecting with a jury is usually easier than it appears. First, as stated above, jurors—up to a point—usually look upon experts as the teachers whom they desperately need. They welcome a tutorial. Second, jurors are not constrained by the subtle nuances we have come to expect in other situations, even in an arbitration setting. Usually, they will nod when they agree with you on a point. Usually they will frown or shake their heads when they disagree. A blank stare from four or more faces tells me that I am not making my point, and it needs a better explanation. So, there are clues when speaking to a jury that are not available to you when facing a professionally indoctrinated stone-faced arbitration panel. (With all due respect to the professionalism of that panel and their ability to tell me little or nothing about what they are hearing or feeling).

Get over any jitters about testifying in front of a crowd. There will be a crowd; depending on the jurisdiction and the type of case, the jury alone is usually twelve people with two alternates, although that also varies depending on the jurisdiction and the type of case. There are usually spectators, sometimes professional spectators, in the courtroom as well, and those spectators are free to come and go at will. There is the judge, who may look bored, but is probably well involved in all aspects of the case. Your focus still must be on your outline, materials, presentation, and equally important, how you connect with these people who will decide your case.

Connecting in front of a jury may not be terribly difficult, but the hard part is how you teach. The jurors will, understandably, not know the subject matter and will have been introduced to the issues and the topics as recently as a few hours earlier.

So, it is a complex process in a very condensed time frame. I have found that the best approach is to step up the beat and your animation a bit. You must make an impression, and being boring is not a winning strategy. Of course, do not overdo it. You are not on stage, but you should imitate the best teacher you ever had. Always maintain eye contact with the jurors, going from one to another, not necessarily sequentially, and I usually give a very subtle nod when making a point. You would be surprised at how many return nods I get.

On cross-examination, the technique is the same as detailed in the cross-examination summary above: Look at opposing counsel when the question is asked, and then pivot your attention to the jury box. Shorter is usually better when speaking with a jury, and work out your testimony with counsel. You may find, as I have done, that a jury trial is an enjoyable and rewarding experience.

As with any testimony, these are suggestions which counsel may want you to modify. Some counsel want you not to interact with the jury, but merely dialogue with counsel. Respect counsel's opinion on these matters.

*     *     *

**A Personal Aside:** *Two jury trials which are illustrative of the above points, one positive and one not so much. In the first, everything I did went according to the book. I connected immediately with the jury on a very complicated hedge fund case wherein the issues were the propriety of a technical non-calculation of margin on a non-traded product. Dry stuff, but the jury seemed to understand the basic arguments we were making of the necessity of trying to value hard-to-value assets. I sensed that the jury understood, the body language spoke volumes, and I got a plethora of head nods and smiles. All went well; the jury quickly returned a favorable verdict.*

*Not so well in the second illustrative case. It was a criminal case, and I never could crack the jury. They were as cold as ice, unresponsive to my testimony and the voluminous amounts of data presented. Perhaps there was too much complex data, but in the end, they were not willing to decide the case on the merits, but rather (according to a survey of the jury after the trial was over) an unwillingness to convict "those nice boys" and those "nicely dressed young men" on criminal fraud charges.*

*The moral? You can do everything right and still struggle to get the intended result. I can only lay out the best path forward. But this is life; sometimes that path takes you over a cliff.*

What about a bench trial, i.e., a trial without a jury in which the judge is both the finder of facts and the decision-maker regarding those facts? You can safely assume that the judge is well-read and conversant on the pretrial briefs and the testimony adduced thus far. Most judges—while their attention may be split between your trial, the motions necessary to be heard in the next trial, and the writing of an opinion on the previous trial—are still devoting most of their energies to what is immediately before them. (Even if it appears that the judge is more focused on reading motions from another matter, give that judge the benefit of the doubt—most judges are born with acute sonar and will perfectly hear live testimony while seemingly doing yesterday's crossword puzzle.)

There is little "manipulating" of a judge. He or she will either connect with you or not. He or she will either accept what you are saying, or not. But the nice thing is that he or she will usually immediately let you know what is troubling to him or her. It is not unusual to have a dialogue with a judge, at the judge's initiation, which might last quite a few minutes. It is a cross-examination without the aggression. That is a wonderful situation, because it clearly indicates two things: First, the judge is involved, and second, the exact nature of a troubling issue is highlighted—and if a troublesome issue is highlighted, it can be addressed.

So, give the judge the deference deserved; do not dumb down the testimony; make your points forcefully but without the touch of drama that might be given to a jury. And always remember that if a judge admonishes you that your point is understood, even if you have more to say, it is a clear indication that no more is necessary. Do not argue. Move on.

* * *

**A Personal Aside:** *In the U.K., there are no jury trials in civil matters; everything is tried before a judge. Furthermore, experts are treated as professionals, no* **ad hominem** *attacks on credentials or credibility. If you are presented as an expert, you are treated as an expert. The goal is to find the truth (shocking!), and therefore, experts are expected to not only write an expert report that serves as the entirety of one's direct testimony, but also to get together with the other expert and prepare a joint report of issues agreed-upon, and issues remaining. Experts are hired by the court (although paid by either side) and are therefore expected to be absolutely neutral in every statement made; no spin, no slanting of the facts or the opinions. No deviation from this neutrality is permitted. In an attempt to be completely deferential to the court, and proud of what I considered to be my total neutrality, I once demurred on a point and stated that an issue under discussion was "up to the court to decide." The judge leaned over to me and said: "Mr. Weiner, what is for the court to decide is up to the court to decide." Fortunately, we both could smile at that exchange, and I moved on.*

## 7 Be Polite, Humble, and Non-Confrontational

It is certainly tempting to fight back and match nasty for nasty when opposing counsel takes off the gloves. Nothing will hurt your case more than going toe-to-toe with opposing counsel on the tone, not the substance, of your testimony. Retain your cool; let your counsel or better yet, the judge or the chairperson, take on the negative atmosphere while you stand above the fray. It will serve you well in the end. It will do you better than that. It leaves you as the adult in the room with opposing counsel having flown off the handle.

But don't expect your counsel to bail you out of an uncomfortable situation. Counsel will do his/her best to run interference for you by objecting to the tone or the substance of the questions, but short of tribal mayhem, triers of fact are reluctant to step into a heated exchange and aid any witness—especially experts who are considered professionals and who do not, or should not, need their assistance. Part of the "game" that counsel and the triers of fact play, cruel as it is, is to see how well a witness stands up to the heat of a contentious cross-examination. This is especially true of expert witnesses. You will have to dig deep into your emotional well and play the game. Remember, it is partially theater, even if it is serious, a-lot-at-stake theater, and you are but another actor in the play.

So continue to answer the questions. Take deep breaths, ignore the personal attacks, and stay focused on your opinions and the facts that support those opinions. Opposing counsel is doing several things: He or she is searching for factual chinks in your opinions and your story, but is also searching for emotional chinks to aid in the unraveling of those opinions and that story.

On a more mundane front, there is a certain majesty about being polite for its own sake, beyond the battle between you and opposing counsel. You should always be deferential to the panel, the judge and the jury. You must refer to everyone in the room by their title: Mr., Ms., or Dr. You should consider being the last to exit the room at a break and the first to re-enter, taking your seat at the witness table or witness box before the rest of your party enters. Recall what was mentioned about being confident and well-dressed, and having a good demeanor. These appear to be trivial things, but will go a long way toward a successful outcome.

One must also be non-confrontational. It is a corollary to being polite. Don't invite confrontation by attacking the opposing expert (as opposed to the flaws contained in the expert's work-product), by impugning the credibility of other witnesses, or by attacking the exhibits of the other side. Your points can be made in a professional manner without inviting the chaos that would follow a confrontation. Let your counsel confront the opposing expert in any manner that he or she deems appropriate; your job is to stay above the fray.

It is perfectly acceptable to dismantle the opposing expert's exhibits with well-reasoned counter arguments regarding validity or relevance; it is not acceptable to call into question the expert's motives, intelligence, or allegiance.

Finally, nothing turns off a jury or an arbitration panel more than cockiness. You can be knowledgeable, somewhat pedantic, and confident while still being humble. I find that a touch of self-deprecating humor goes a long way.

* * *

**A Personal Aside:** *Opposing experts (three of them), well-credentialed, had gone on for four days spinning elaborate tales of malfeasance, injustice, injury, and ineptitude, using intricate and unique theories on trading norms, nuances, and nonsense. It was, to me, a breathtaking diversion from the real issues in the case, and a smokescreen unlike any I had seen before. They asked the panel to accept as fact (and law) that which was only hypothetical theory at best and fantasy at worst.*

*My rebuttal was relatively easy and took less than an hour: I used, sequentially, each of their many, many assertions, and pointed out carefully, firmly, and in a non-confrontational manner, that there was no justification in any law, rule, book, treatise, or industry custom or practice to accept this point and the next point, and the next point. When I was finished, I summarized in so many words that: "This was the experts' case: None of it matters; it might all be true, it isn't—but even if it were—it doesn't matter, since it is completely irrelevant to the issues before you." I then proceeded with an overview of my opinions, making sure that they were far more succinct and totally relevant to the issues.*

*There are three morals to this tale: First, elaborate smoke-screens generally will not work (in the above case, the panel quickly rejected the claimant's expert arguments in their entirety). Factfinders will see through them, resent them, and rebuff them. Second, you can dissect opposing experts by using their own words and theories against them—just do it in a polite, non-confrontational manner. Finally, many of the most effective defense expert presentations are fashioned only after the claimant or plaintiff expert case is presented. This requires deftness and a lot of late nights, but can be strikingly effective.*

## 8 Be a Good Listener—or "Just Answer the Question"

Listen hard and well. When testifying, answer **exactly** the question asked, and unless, on cross-examination where you are certain that you have been afforded the opportunity to hit an all-but-guaranteed home run, resist the temptation to elaborate beyond the precise boundaries of the question.

A lawyer I've known for years uses the following to illustrate the issue to his prospective witnesses:

*Lawyer: "Do you have the time?"*

*Witness: "It's 10 to 3."*

*Lawyer: "No! The answer to my question is 'Yes.'"*

Think about that question and answer. It is accurate, it is precise, it answers the question, it should not be considered offensive, and it causes opposing counsel to dig deeper. As I mentioned earlier, I was once given the admonition regarding opposing counsel to "Make this the worst day of his life." I do not actually believe that to be a good or even realistic strategy, but if there is any good take-away from that advice, it may be "Don't give opposing counsel a gift; answer only the question asked."

You must assume that counsel—your counsel and opposing counsel—fashion their questions precisely. That is what is taught at the very expensive laws schools from which they presumably graduated. So, the questions must be answered with the same precision: Answer only the question asked, no more, no less, and certainly without moving onto a tangent that was not requested. If you stray into new areas with an imprecise answer, all that you have done is open new avenues for opposing counsel to explore. You have done this to yourself. Maybe he or she was going to get there eventually, or maybe not. Maybe that area was not even relevant and/or admissible. But with your careless or imprecise answer, you literally opened a legal door for exploration of the subject matter. Don't do it.

A favorite lawyer for whom I used to work would grill his own witnesses before a hearing or a trial and invariably, repeatedly, and stridently, would bellow, "Answer the damn question" to his now-cowering soon-to-be witness. It was never (or rarely) that the witness was trying to be evasive, but it is an art form to be able to listen, understand, process, and *only then*, speak well. But that is exactly what is necessary: Listen, understand, process and speak well.

The trick often taught by experienced counsel to novice witnesses is to hesitate slightly before answering. It reinforces the listening process, aids in the comprehension, allows for a more reasoned response and, counsel hopes, leads to a better, more accurate answer.

And that, dear friends, is **ESSENTIAL RULE NUMBER FIVE: Listen, understand, process, hesitate, and only then, speak.**

• • •

**A Personal Aside:** *The opposing expert was on cross-examination, explaining how a graph came to be. In answer to a question regarding the date stamp on the bottom of the exhibit,* *to wit: "What is the meaning of that date?" he shockingly explained: "That is the date that we finally got the result we were looking for; there were so many other attempts and drafts that preceded that date."*

*No. The proper answer to the question should have been: "That was the date of the production of this graph." Would counsel have dug deeper and elicited that there were numerous attempts to construct an acceptable graphic? Perhaps, but please do not ever hand counsel such a gift-wrapped nugget.*

Incidentally, this advice to listen carefully is also applicable to questions asked on direct examination and questions from the bench and/or the arbitration panel. The most common reaction by a trier of fact to an answer that does not address the question, or is only tangentially related, is annoyance, and annoyance leads to loss of credibility. I have heard too many admonitions for a witness to "Please, just answer the question; listen to the question and answer it."

How many times have we watched a politician being interviewed by a journalist after which we muse: "He never did answer the question." That may be good political theater; it is a skill learned through experience, and it may provide cover for that politician, but it is anathema in a litigation setting. It is the least desirable mode of handling oneself in litigation.

This advice also pertains to your relationship with counsel in a pre-litigation setting. In your early conversations, listen carefully to what counsel desires of you. It will form the core of your ongoing relationship and will provide the framework for your opinions, your demonstratives, your exhibits, the scope of your research, and the degree of depth of preparation expected of you. If you "get it wrong," your relationship may not be terminal, especially if any misunderstanding occurs early in the relationship, but it is critical to get off on the right foot, and that requires that you listen well.

• • •

**Note:** *In a pre-litigation setting, should you take notes during or immediately after speaking with counsel? Should you send counsel confirming e-mails? Should you continue to communicate through e-mails? Those are not easy questions to answer. Some counsel prefer that there be no paper trail reflecting conversations between counsel and testifying expert since there is no attorney-client privilege—or any other privilege that would attach to those conversations. Other counsel would rather that you get your assignment as requested and have a good and ongoing dialogue, and therefore would allow notetaking and e-mails.*

*The latest amendments to the federal rules concerning experts do provide some protection, e.g., drafts of expert reports are no longer discoverable, but the language is not all-inclusive. The best advice is twofold: First, check with counsel during your very first conversation to see his or her preferred method of handling this issue; and second, if notetaking and e-mails are acceptable to counsel, think long and hard about what goes into them—the best defense is to assume that opposing counsel will eventually have access to them and will cross- examine you on each of your entries.*

**Another Personal Aside:** *I was interviewing a prospective expert on behalf of my company and gave the individual the relevant agreed-upon defenses in an extensive series of forthcoming cases about to be fully litigated. The prospect* *was being presented an opportunity to lighten my workload and take many of the matters from me—to the prospect's great financial advantage. But the prospective expert could not focus on discussing the defenses at hand and instead fervently maintained and insisted that no firm that sold these products could possibly be defended. No matter how many times I tried to move the conversation back to the issues and the defenses, there was another non-responsive answer. The prospect did not get the assignment because it was proven that listening was not that person's strong suit. (Also, this prospective expert was clearly better suited to the claimant/ plaintiff side in these matters).*

## 9 Be Candid

No case and no fact pattern are perfect. If you admit the shortcomings of the situation, or of the underlying facts that form the basis of your opinions, you are far better off than trying to rationalize and explain. Get any uncomfortable situation out of the way on direct examination. Demonstrate that, notwithstanding those shortcomings, your opinions are solid and you will be far more credible. Of course, you will be cross-examined on those shortcomings, but you will be well-prepared for that cross, and the result is you will develop a credibility with the triers of fact that far exceeds the alternative strategy of denying any weakness.

For example, when presenting data in a chart or a graph, if one or more data points are statistically unreliable, I immediately point those out during my direct examination. (They are also so noted on the exhibit for the same reason.) I follow up by stating that those data points do not invalidate either the theory or the exhibit and explain the reasons why that is so. Because the exhibit is proactively marked with numerous footnotes—including one that points out this shortcoming—testifying to it on direct examination takes the wind out of opposing counsel's sails. In fact, you can actually see the disappointment on counsel's face.

From that point forward, there is not a cloud on your testimony or on your reputation, and the testimony that will follow will be substantially more credible.

• • •

**A Personal Aside:** *It is a torturous and most uncomfortable scene to watch a fellow expert witness try to deny the obvious. In a recent hearing, an expert tried to claim that futures contracts were invalid as a matter of law and public policy because they constituted gambling. The testimony was patently absurd for a multitude of reasons, paramount of which was that futures trading continues to have the imprimatur of approval by the federal government through the Commodity Exchange Act and furthermore, that identical argument had been tried and rejected by federal courts many years ago. And yet, the expert, using discredited theories and ancient treatises, maintained that the contracts were null and void, and his client should not have to pay a six-figure debit. The arbitration panel disagreed.*

*There was no good reason why that case should have been tried, and if it were to be tried, a more plausible defense should have been offered. The debit was clearly owed, and if there were any reasonable defenses, they were not advanced by the expert witness. By failing to acknowledge the obvious, the expert obliterated his reputation and failed to assist his client.*

**Another Personal Aside:** *A complex options case was being arbitrated in New York wherein the claimant's expert presented a detailed and complex calculation on damages. There was one problem: It was mathematically incorrect. Since exhibits must be turned over to the other side 20 days before a hearing, we had the opportunity to test his calculations and discovered his error. Even if one accepted his theory of damages (which was relatively bizarre), if that theory had been properly calculated, there would have been no damages. We pointed this out on cross-examination, but the expert refused to admit to his error. As often as we recalculated and pointed out the error in both logic and mathematics, the expert dug deeper into the validity of his work product.*

*After a while, the arbitration chair, mercifully, asked opposing counsel if he would like to take a break to discuss this matter with his expert and his client. It was a clear signal that the arbitration was over, and it was. The claimant withdrew his claim.*

On a related point, if there is something you simply don't know, say so. Be upfront. Perhaps you might want to ruminate for a few seconds, but be aware: There is nothing more pathetic than an expert who is clearly trying to obscure the fact that he/she simply does not know the answer to a question. Never fake it; never lie. Again, fact witnesses are always told by counsel that "I don't know" or "I don't remember" are perfectly acceptable answers. Experts can take a cue from that advice, although it is to be hoped that the demurs should be infrequent and not in the areas of the professed expertise.

## 10 Be a Touch Pedantic

You want to teach, you need to teach, but you are not giving a lecture to a graduate class, because that would be too pedantic. Nor are you giving a lecture to a high school class; that would be too condescending. You must learn how to teach the material you are presenting to the expectations of an arbitration panel or a judge or a jury.

They do not expect a strictly academic lecture, even though, at the outset, many panelists and juries are grateful for someone to explain and synthesize, in simple terms, what has been previously presented by numerous witnesses. I have seen good success by an academic giving a limited lecture on the finer points of an issue. The problem comes with scale: a full-throated college lecture has diminishing returns even though it can convey a wealth of knowledge.

Nothing will enthrall a panel or a jury more than the first 10 minutes of a well-constructed lecture—and nothing will turn them off more than the next 20, 30 or 40 minutes of that same lecture. Know when to stop. Know when to have counsel break up your testimony, ease up, and when to take a break. Don't ever treat your audience as if it is ignorant, and never be condescending.

Your primary job is to teach—to explain why the opinions that you are offering are proper, fit the fact patterns, and are intellectually honest. Despite the warnings not to be too pedantic, you must consider yourself to be a teacher. But be cognizant of your audience and their reactions to you and your material.

I have often found that counsel can help break up a long presentation by interjecting a probing question or two. It works better than a continuing monologue and seems less like the Finance 101 lecture you do want, but really must avoid. It is far better to do it with counsel asking questions than to stop and inquire if the panel, judge, or the jury is still "with me?"

In being (a touch) pedantic, it helps greatly in keeping the attention of your audience by referring to visuals, to reference your exhibits, and to subtly involving the audience in your presentation.

You do not have to go as far as asking if they understand—your job is not to ask questions—but to be adept at reading their reactions. How? When moving from exhibit to exhibit, are they following your lead? When the exhibit is opened, do they scan it? Do they appear to understand it? Your job is to make sure that they do understand it on two levels: first, understand the document itself and second, understand the relevance vis à vis your opinion.

It is often said that a good defense expert is really giving an advance of counsel's closing argument. That is absolutely correct. You can be a tremendous aid to counsel by fashioning your testimony as a lesson which hits the highlights of counsel's opening statement, and thus serves as a preview to the closing statement. That only works, of course, if the opinions that you were hired to give are broad enough to serve the purpose of previewing counsel's close.

* * *

**A Personal Aside:** *An expert believes himself to be "the smartest person in the room" (He once actually said to an arbitration panel: "Since clearly I'm the only one here who understands this issue, let me try again. Please do listen.")*

*That expert's testimony was not only thoroughly pedantic,*

*but also completely condescending, as if teaching a class of underachievers who need to know the information but are incapable of truly understanding it. For the first 15 or 20 minutes, the panel or the jury is enthralled. But the lecture never ends; and it is completely patronizing. Sooner or later—mostly sooner, the panel turns on that expert, and by the end of the testimony the panelists either ignore every point the expert was trying to make, or intensely dislike the personality, or both. I've seen it happen countless number of times.*

**Another Personal Aside:** *Another expert is an academic who testifies exactly as if giving a college lecture. He is likeable, knowledgeable, but has two flaws that often hurt his credibility: First, the bias in the testimony (not the lack of independence, just bias towards one side of the retail securities universe) is so blatant that the lecture turns into an infomercial for his point of view. Second, there are a lack of detail and flaws in reasoning that very often unravel the expert's opinions during cross-examination. If the testimony, even as a college lecture, is not internally consistent with the facts as presented, it will not stand the scrutiny of cross-examination.*

Therefore, go ahead and teach and be a bit pedantic. But once the learning curve kicks in, it should lead you to the proper balance between lecture and testimony. There is a difference.

## 11 I Am Not a Lawyer, But...

One other aspect of effective testimony is tricky to master: inserting oneself into the legal arguments, applying the facts to the law. It is tricky because you are, most likely, not a lawyer, and even if you are, you are not acting as such in this situation. And yet, you are an expert in the field; you constantly applied the industry rules and standards to the factual situations that you dealt with daily when you were an industry leader. Perhaps you even had a hand in creating internal or even industry standards. So why not interpret the facts at issue to the law, and to the rules and regulations that guide the industry?

There are several answers, and many more pitfalls. First, your counsel may not want you to go there, instead wanting to save the "legal arguments" for his or her closing statements. Second, opposing counsel will surely object stating that you are not a lawyer and have no standing to interpret the law, rules or regulations. Third, the arbitration panel or the judge may object and deny the testimony on the basis that legal conclusions are not in the province of expert testimony.

Obviously, some fiction is at play, and there is a dance that will be going on. If counsel strongly desires your testimony on those points, he or she will make the argument (as should you, if asked) that the practical experience of applying "the law to the facts" is what you did on a daily basis, and testimony should be allowed to aid the panel or the judge in determining how the industry applies "the law" to any given factual situation.

* * *

**A Personal Aside:** *For many years, I was able to testify to the law largely because of my legal and regulatory background. I was counsel to two major financial institutions, helped formulate industry regulations, and prior to that worked for a governmental agency with jurisdiction over many of* *the matters at issue. That experience often seemed to trump any objections that legal testimony should not come from expert witnesses. However, in a number of cases where legal testimony was denied, I found it quite easy to reformulate my testimony from the legal to the "industry practice." In other words, the testimony did not rely on the letter of the law, but on how the industry interpreted its requirements—essentially the same thing, but in a less objectionable manner. It is almost impossible for opposing counsel to object to illustrations of an industry expert explaining industry practice. That is why you are testifying!*

This is one area where you, as an expert, must clarify the testimony with counsel well in advance and have a strategy to get the necessary testimony admitted.

So, at long last, incorporating all the above, having examined the essential elements of being an effective testifying expert witness in the financial services area, let me propose perhaps the most critical of the essential rules—**ESSENTIAL RULE NUMBER SIX: No one should attempt to testify—or even consult—if there is even the slightest uncertainty regarding one's expertise.**

I am going to assume that you, the reader, are intelligent, well-read, and articulate. I will concede that you are, in fact, a subject- matter expert in your field and have had a remarkable career in the financial services industry. But I also recognize that no one is an expert in all aspects of a given subject, even within the broader range of the recognized expertise. Therefore, once again, **no one should attempt to testify if there is even the slightest uncertainty regarding one's expertise in the subject matter offered for opinion testimony.** This is no time to be a hero and extend yourself beyond your comfort zone. This is no time to stretch.

Listen to your inner self and be pro-active: Discuss the "fit" with counsel, do it sooner rather than later, long before you take the stand, and if you determine that an area is beyond your expertise, or even outside your comfort zone, develop a means to maintain your value to counsel without testifying to areas where you lack the necessary credentials.

If you cannot testify to X, Y and Z, perhaps you are still valuable in testifying to A, B, and C. Perhaps you can be of service by testifying only to data and the resultant exhibits. Perhaps you can move into a consulting role with another expert. Counsel, most likely, will still desire your expertise, but the last thing counsel needs is to have you (and therefore his or her case) subject to effective attack (through the *voir dire* process) before substantive testimony even begins.

Following the *voir dire*, even if the judge or the panel ultimately allows your testimony to proceed, if opposing counsel has mounted an effective challenge to your credentials, there will be damage done to your client's case, even if that damage is not substantive. Even if it is only psychological, it inflicts a pall over the entirety of your direct testimony and you can expect to see many more negative comments regarding credentials during cross-examination.

It is essential to be offered for testimony in only those areas in which your credentials are beyond reproach. You must be proactive and nip any controversy in the bud by communicating with counsel early and often regarding your expertise and the areas in which you will be offered as an expert.

&#42; &#42; &#42;

**A Personal Aside:** *My career as an expert began in the early 1990's; the plaintiff's bar was not well-organized, had little expertise or understanding of the nuances of a securities fraud case, and relied on experts who, with few exceptions, contributed little to a trier of fact's understanding of the issues. In that milieu, it was easy to "stretch" and become an expert in tangential areas just beyond my "sweet spot." But as the years rolled on, even though my testimonial skills increased, so did the understanding of all the issues and their nuances by opposing counsel. It was harder to fit my expertise into all related areas. I began to sweat the voir dire; my challenges became more extensive and effective. And while I was never denied or limited in my testimony, before that could happen, I took the affirmative step of limiting my assignments to those areas in which I was comfortable. It helped me, it helped counsel, it helped my clients.*

We will explore *voir dire* more fully later in this book, but be assured that it is highly critical to a successful career to have no blemishes—zero, not even one, on one's testimonial history and to be able to truthfully answer the following *voir dire* questions in the negative: "Have you ever been denied the opportunity to testify?" "Has any of your previous testimony ever been limited in scope by a court or an arbitration panel?"

An affirmative answer to either of those questions, especially the first, can seriously damage your ongoing prospects as a testifying expert. Counsel has the right to be choosy; you are not irreplaceable and many attorneys consider affirmative answers to the questions regarding past limitations on testimony to be a litmus test for engagement.

The take-away is simply that your proposed testimony

should be squarely and demonstratively in line with your expertise, and you and counsel must agree precisely on what the scope of your testimony will be. Then, at trial or at an arbitration hearing, there will be no question regarding your expertise vis à vis the issues at hand.

# CHAPTER THREE

# ANSWERING THE CALL

*The First Interview with a Potential Client or "Please Hire Me!"*

When answering a call from counsel for a potential expert witness assignment, understand that you are being interviewed for two things: your subject-matter knowledge and your "fit." The interview will concentrate on these two areas, which are intertwined. You will not be moving back and forth between them, but rather, demonstrating your knowledge while laying out the case as to why you, as an expert, fit into counsel's vision for a successful outcome in the matter.

It is essential to be candid with counsel; there must be no surprises about who you are. While otherwise extoling your virtues, at an early opportune time, you must relate to counsel the following information:

- Your detailed experience that is similar to the issues at hand, including all relevant time frames to allow counsel to judge whether your experience is, perhaps, too old or too shallow;

- Your subject-knowledge background, i.e., how did you obtain your knowledge. Some such background might be problematic if it is too imprecise, too shallow, or too old;

- Your testimonial experience, i.e., whether you have ever testified before, how many times you have testified, the forums in which you have testified, and whether you have ever had consulting assignments in the securities industry;

- Whether any transcripts of your prior testimonies are available to counsel;

- Whether any court or arbitration panel have imposed limits on your testimony or denied you the opportunity to testify;

- Whether you have had any run-ins with the law, federal, state or local, no matter the resolution, regardless of how old or how seemingly insignificant;

- Which licenses you hold (or have held) in the securities industry and whether there are any "dings" on those licenses from FINRA or any other professional body, regardless of resolution or timeframe;

- Whether you have received any professional reprimands, e.g., from a previous employer;

- Whether any potential conflicts of interest emanate from the parties and witnesses known to you at this time;

- Whether any medical issues might impair your ability to perform your professional tasks;

- Whether any limitations on your time exist, especially if you maintain employment while simultaneously acting as an expert witness, and what priority will be given to the prospective matter at hand in the event of a conflict;

- Whether any limitations exist on your ability to research or to produce exhibits;

Be proactive. It is better to be upfront about all issues, including possible negative ones, than to cause counsel to regret having asked you in the interview process.

Once those issues are out of the way, the discussion should turn to the specifics of your background as found in your C.V.

## YOUR C.V.

Counsel should have your C.V. (*curriculum vitae*, also known as your résumé, but in business, the term C.V. is most often used) in front of him or her, so make sure that it is perfect; bulletproof.

Work long and hard to perfect your C.V. Remember, your C.V. will later, at a trial or a deposition, be scrutinized by opposing counsel and picked over word for word and used in your cross-examination and/or your *voir dire*. You must be able not only to defend and explain every entry, but also to be factually certain of items such as:

- Every date of employment;
- Every title you held and the dates those titles were applicable;
- The reason(s) that you changed employment;
- The FINRA tests you took and their dates (and if your licenses have expired following the two-year grace period—say so);
- The number of employees supervised;

- The names and titles of your supervisors;
- Every address of every office you resided in and the number of employees in those offices;
- The name of the colleges you attended, the dates that you attended, the degrees earned, and the dates that they were received;
- Any other higher education credits received, including relevant seminars attended, whether sponsored by your employer or otherwise;
- Your testimonial history;
- Your professional duties and how they changed over time.

Your C.V. must also be complete. Later in the process, opposing counsel will seize on any missing time periods and drill down with you on where you were, what you were doing, and why there is a gap in your life's presentation. If you took any time away from your professional life, if there are any gaps at all, you must include them on your C.V. You should also consider including uncomfortable items such as arrests, criminal convictions, suspensions from securities-related employments or suspension or revocation of securities licenses. Those items will be on your FINRA background check (assuming you are or were FINRA- registered), available to the public, so be aware that with a minimal amount of checking (and opposing counsel will absolutely do at least the minimum amount of checking), opposing counsel will already know the answers to the questions about to be asked.

During the interview process, far friendlier than a *voir dire*, with a far friendlier counsel deciding whether to hire you, the above admonitions may not be as critical, but why not have your bulletproof C.V. ready to present to all who are interested in your background?

At a later trial, deposition, or hearing, some of the cross-examination or *voir dire* questions based upon your C.V. will be petty, partially in an attempt to rattle you or throw you off your game. But know that every question and answer duo leaves an impression, and you have an opportunity to shine by deflecting an attack question of your professional history into a hardening of your professional qualifications.

• • •

**A Personal Aside:** *Too many times I have witnessed what I consider to be a sham scuffle over, believe it or not, a witness's name and the status of licenses held:*

> "Are you Richard D. Jones or Rick Jones? Are you R. David Jones? Are you the same Rickey Jones that had a DUI in 1992 in Dearborn, Michigan? Are you the Rich Jones who was suspended by the S.E.C. in 2001 for failing to pay a reparations award? Are you changing identities because you have something to hide?"

> "You state you have FINRA licenses 3,4,8,9,10,22, and 24. But isn't it a fact that your licenses have expired since you are no longer affiliated with a broker-dealer for a period of two years, and therefore your attestation to this panel is misleading?"

*Counsel knows perfectly well the answers to these questions. They are mean, petty and not designed to elicit any meaningful information. The line of questioning should be cut off and counsel admonished, but often is not. Those questions are designed to intimidate or embarrass and nothing else, but, again, I have witnessed it too often, and it tests a witness' resolve and concentration.*

But the salient point is that your C.V. is, from a litigation viewpoint, you. You must own it; it must tell your story; and it must be totally accurate and complete. Before you begin your testimony, and while you are being qualified as an expert, a judge or an arbitration panel will be studying your C.V. and forming opinions of you.

There are volumes available on the internet as to how to create an effective C.V., but only four salient points are to be made as to how to do so. Above and beyond that, your C.V. should be accurate and complete.

First, I suggest having several variations prepared, each of which highlights a particular skill set. For example, if you are interviewing for a position that requires expertise in the margining of options, I would lead off your "Summary" section with a note that highlights your experience in back office supervision of options, which, of course, includes the margining of those options. Thereafter, in reciting your lengthy and deep experience in all things financial, emphasize the options component whenever possible. In another situation, for example, one that requires supervisory skills, the emphasis should be on the length and depth of your experience as a supervisor. It is only a matter of emphasis; your C.V. should always reflect the totality of your experience.

*   *   *

**Cautionary Note:** *Your C.V. will follow you from case to case. Opposing counsel will quickly notice the fact that your current*

*C.V. is not identical to that which was used a few months ago. Be totally honest: State that the information is the same, but emphasis is placed on the relevant areas of expertise that the panel or the court may find to be of most use.*

Second, make your C.V. easy to follow. A summary section might lead it off, followed by your post-high school education, followed by your employment history (in significant detail with firm name, dates, places, responsibilities, office locales, number of subordinates, and so forth), ending perhaps with a section on publications, honors, awards, FINRA exams passed, and additional education. Omit any mention of references: That is unnecessary and meaningless in this setting. Later, with increased experience, you can add a section on your engagement and testimonial history, being as specific as you deem necessary while keeping in mind the confidentiality of certain proceedings and settlements.

I often will omit names and case numbers on arbitrations (again, which are non-public) and settled matters that have confidentiality agreements, but it depends on the use and purpose of the C.V.: if it is only for counsel's use, eyes-only, I will give full details. However, if it is for wider distribution purposes, I will mask the identities as necessary.

Third, while keeping in mind all that I said about "You are your C.V.," try to keep your C.V. to no more than three, maybe four, pages. Yes, I know, you are accomplished and have a lot of experience to impart. And yes, you are now cognizant of being complete, but unless you are an academic, within the bounds of said completeness, brevity is important. You might score a few points with a long and detailed résumé, but you will also lose your readers after page three. I know it is a bit of a tightrope walk trying to include all relevant information while keeping a C.V. to a reasonable length, but the only way to figure it out it is to start drafting the document.

It is also significant, and might be helpful to remember your audience. If you are drafting a résumé strictly for the use by counsel, for interview purposes only, then there is no reason to be constrained. Go ahead and tell your story. If, however, it will be used in a litigation setting, I prefer a more streamlined version—always remembering the caution for completeness.

The academic C.V. is the exception to this rule. The typical academic C.V. might run 30 or 40 pages or more and include scores and scores of publications, lectures and testimonies given in great detail. But not to worry, you are not in a competition for C.V. length—but rather for relevant experience. An academic approach is one method of trying to convince a trier of fact of relevant experience, but industry experience is certainly on equal footing.

*  *  *

**A Personal Aside:** *The first time I was opposed by an expert witness/professor with a 37-page C.V., I was duly intimidated. He certainly had the history of publications in the general area of securities, and had testified numerous times, but when one drilled down into his qualifications, the qualifications were all academic; he had not spent a minute working in the industry and the voir dire fully exposed that point. There is, of course, nothing wrong with that, but a panel or a jury must decide which experience is more relevant; perhaps they are of equal importance, but I did learn that there is no need to be intimidated.*

Fourth, your C.V. should include no gimmicks. No pictures, no fancy typeface, no colors, limited bold type or italics, just plain white paper. Why? Because it's simple and professional looking.

## Your Interview

You will be quizzed on your knowledge of the subject matter, most likely generically, since counsel has probably not provided you with any pleadings. In most cases, just the outline of a case will be presented, enough to filter out those potential experts who have no expertise in the particular field. In other cases, especially large, complex matters, counsel may be interviewing you, but leaving open the possibility that a rather broad mix of experts, working in concert, may fit counsel's needs. In a sense, counsel is fishing for what might become a team of experts in a complicated matter. Note that in complex litigation matters, it is not unusual for two or more experts to testify on behalf of a single litigant.

## Interview Preparation

If possible, long before the interview, ask to see the pleadings. This serves two purposes: First, the pleadings give you a broader, more in-depth understanding of the case and will put you in a far better position to understand the issues, and allows you time to formulate potential opinions and ask relevant, probing questions. Second, it shows initiative and drive. Generally, nothing impresses counsel more than a potential expert who is willing to dig deep and understand the case even when no compensation is involved (and you WILL NOT charge for that time spent preparing for the interview, even if you later get the assignment.)

•  •  •

**Note:** *Even if counsel has not provided the pleadings, if the matter has been filed in court, they are available publicly, in an electronic format. Get them and study them. There is really no reason not to have looked at the publicly available documents, but this does not apply to arbitration filings, which are confidential in nature and available only through counsel.*

If pleadings are not available, that may put you in a somewhat vulnerable position. Sometimes that is exactly what counsel wants. But to have a productive discussion, it is essential that you understand the outlines of counsel's case. So, it is incumbent upon you to ask the following relevant questions early in the discussion:

- What are the salient facts?
- What are the issues that counsel sees?
- What particular expertise is being sought?
- What statutes, regulations, rules, customs and practices will be at issue?
- What opinions, on a preliminary basis, does counsel see being offered?
- What are the strengths and weaknesses of the case?
- At what stage is the litigation?
- How do you see that I, or my associates, can be of assistance?
- What is the need for any demonstrative exhibits?

Despite asking the relevant centering questions, above, do not try to pretend to understand the case. You do not.

Counsel does. Instead, stick to your expertise, show counsel that you are an expert in the areas in which he or she needs help. Phrase answers in the hypothetical using your knowledge of the industry, e.g., "If X did, in fact, do so, I'm sure you are aware of the section of the FINRA rules that states. … We can certainly illustrate those facts for the panel by using our standard XYZ model."

And now is the time to recall an earlier admonition:

**Always remember Essential Rule Number Six: "No one should attempt to testify if there is even the slightest uncertainty regarding one's expertise in the subject matter of opinion testimony."** If, after listening to counsel, you believe that this case stretches your expertise, remember this important rule.

The second reason you are being interviewed is for "the fit." This is where you will be selling yourself as both an expert and as an individual. So, the question is: "How do I present myself and my credentials independently of the facts of this case?" These questions are vital not only for the pre-hire interview, but will be critical in the hearing/trial setting when you are asked to explain to the panel or the court your qualifications to testify as an expert. The following is perhaps more pertinent to the litigation setting than an interview, but the principles are the same, and you can always adopt a less formal approach for the interview.

**ESSENTIAL RULE NUMBER SEVEN: Practice, Practice, Practice Your Qualifications.**

There are very few things one needs to memorize in the field of expert witnessing other than one's qualifications. But the qualifications are vital to your credibility with a prospective employer as well as with the trier of facts. You need to be proficient regarding your background and how it fits into the factual setting you find yourself. You should be thorough, clear, and confident. You need to sit down in front of a mirror and tell your story, again, and again until it is perfect.

The narrative of your qualifications can parallel your C.V., but do not read it; counsel will have it in front of him or her. Expand on it, use different phrases and enlighten counsel even though your C.V. may be the basis of the initial discussion.

After introducing yourself to the prospective client (or, later, to an arbitration panel or to the court), you should begin with an overview of your experience, e.g., "I have spent 30 years as a supervisor, with increasing responsibilities, with two of the largest national wirehouses, in the fields of margin and credit review—areas directly pertinent to the issues before this body. ..." This overview cannot be overstated. This is the entrée into credibility for everything that follows.

While it is an overview, it is also the paramount reason why you should be hired; and in the case of testimony, why you should be given deference. Obviously, this overview will change from assignment to assignment because the focus of the assignments differs; your qualifications should (only if they are so capable) match those changes.

Next, state your collegiate education, giving degrees obtained and the year degrees were earned. Any other relevant educational information, such as seminars and workshops should also be stated.

Then move on to a chronological review of your career path. Hit the highlights, but do not feel pressured to short-change yourself. You are selling yourself. You are telling your story. It is a critical moment in both the interview and the testimonial situations.

● ● ●

**Note:** *Consider raising the possibility of a video conference interview. It holds its own challenges for the camera-shy (but should you be in this business if you are camera-shy?). If you're intimidated speaking in front of a camera, consider overcoming your fear. There is no shortage of books about how to speak in front of a camera, and there are also coaches who'll work with you one-on-one until you're comfortable being yourself with a camera and microphone recording your every movement. It's worth the extra effort, because the benefits are tremendous.*

*Assuming you have the personality for this profession (I will discuss that later), why not ask to show it off and interact with counsel while seeing each other? I much preferred that format over a telephone call with an unfamiliar attorney. It's a true ice-breaker and leads to better discussions. These days, video conference facilities are everywhere and the cost is de minimis.*

**A Personal Aside:** *There is a fine line between just enough and too much detail. My "background testimony," wherein I introduced myself at a hearing or trial, usually took about 15 to 20 minutes, depending on the type of case. Sometimes it was important to detail the prowess of the back office of my firm. Sometimes the experience gained as an owner of a broker-dealer was important, sometimes not. The same applies to my testimony history. But I have seen experts who spent the greater part of an arbitration morning on background—far*

*too much information. Invariably the point of diminishing*
*returns occurs at about the 20-minute mark.*

**Note:** *You should begin to develop a "Testimonial History"*
*as a supplement to your C.V. (Until it gets too lengthy, it*
*can simply be a part of the C.V. itself). It will be submit-*
*ted to opposing counsel along with your primary C.V. I*
*developed two versions: One has all information regarding*
*the cases where testimony was given including the case*
*name and number, the date of my testimony, the forum,*
*the city where the matter was litigated, the party on behalf*
*of which I testified, and a concise summary of the issues.*
*Never declare the outcome—experts are supposed to be*
*neutral and not care who wins—just a professional stating*
*unbiased opinions.*

*The second is a truncated version, which omits the case*
*name and number, substituting "a national brokerage firm"*
*or a "regional brokerage firm" for the institutional party and*
*XYZ for the individuals. I find that version more suitable for*
*turnover to opposing counsel as it not only preserves the con-*
*fidentiality of the parties, but also tends to obscure questions*
*on concentration of clients—a potential matter of conflict of*
*interest or of independence.*

*In federal court, the rules state that testimonial history*
*going back five years must be provided—so the full version is*
*submitted. Some counsel want me to cut it off at the five-year*
*mark and some feel the rule requests a minimum submission,*
*so the full document going back to my testimonial beginning*
*is offered. In the arbitration setting, I usually (but not always)*
*submitted the redacted version to avoid questions on potential*
*bias stemming from assignments emanating from one or more*
*major clients. This is another matter to be discussed, well in*

*advance, with counsel.*

Of course, doing everything correctly, nailing your background, expressing amazing knowledge of the subject matter does not assure a successful "fit." There are the intangibles that one cannot prepare for, such as counsel's "feeling" that you may not be the right candidate for the assignment. Fear not and trudge along—there will be other cases, with the same attorney or others, and be assured that if you have done all well, a callback may be in your future. (And remember this important aside: I'm not your mother, but do send counsel a thank you note.)

* * *

**Note:** *There is little useful advice on how to overcome the very real hurdle of being a testimonial virgin. Counsel, understandably, would prefer a known quantity, one who has been tested under the fires and rigors of cross-examination. However, several areas may be of possible assistance:*

> *First, try hard for the "easier" or lower-dollar cases where counsel may be more willing to break in a new expert.*
>
> *Second, gather as many references as you can regarding both your experience and your character to assuage any fears. Offer these, verbally, to counsel. Counsel will need persuading, but may also recognize that you are worth the gamble if he or she can be convinced that you are worth the risk. Yes, it is a risk, so try to understand counsel's reluctance.*
>
> *Third, be up front; tell counsel at the outset that you have not yet testified but that you are well-versed in both the subject matter and the process.*

*Fourth, be prepared for disappointment. There will be times, perhaps most of the times, where counsel is just not prepared to go with an inexperienced, untested expert. But keep going, keep interviewing, keep trying. Your time will come.*

# CHAPTER FOUR

# I'VE BEEN HIRED

*Now What?*

Now the real fun begins. Counsel says, "You're the (wo) man," and he/she indicates that you will be his/her testifying expert witness in his litigation matter. Now what?

**Housekeeping**

**ESSENTIAL RULE NUMBER EIGHT: These Little Housekeeping Matters Are Your Lifeblood—Please Do It Right!**

First, are you being hired through a firm or on your own? If through a firm, it will undoubtedly have the proper forms to sign, which includes, most importantly, the Retainer Agreement. That agreement sets forth the terms and conditions of your relationship with counsel and his/her client. It is a critical document: Among other things, it confirms exactly who has hired you. Is it the law firm or is it the client? The difference is significant and will play a critical role if push ever comes to shove regarding payment disputes. Also, very often, I have been asked during a hearing or a trial, "Who is your client?" The answer lies within the pages of your Retainer Agreement.

* * *

**A Personal Aside:** *In my 20-plus years of doing expert work, I have never been "stiffed" by a client—until my penultimate assignment where I felt sorry for an individual plaintiff who was clearly wronged by a very bad and shameless broker. My assignment was huge: Two expert reports in federal court, a deposition, testimony in federal court, writing cross-examination for the opposing expert, and writing my own direct examination. I paid little attention to either the Retainer Agreement, the retainer itself, or to the unpaid bills. I never should have gone to testify with such large mid-five figure unpaid invoices—invoices which, to this day, remain unpaid despite a successful outcome to the litigation. Do as I say, not as I do: Do not let things get out of hand. Getting paid is not optional, and you are not a charity. Do as I say. ...*

If you are on your own, without a firm to provide guidance, I urge you to research and adopt (or better yet, adapt) a Retainer Agreement that can be found all over the internet.

Counsel will often have an agreement of his/her own ready for you to sign. Be careful. While there is nothing nefarious about signing someone else's agreement, read it very carefully. Undoubtedly, it will indicate that you are being hired by the litigant, not counsel, and the litigant is responsible for all payments. As a former law firm partner, I can certainly understand that: Lawyers are not in the business of guaranteeing payments to third parties. But if you can (and admittedly, it is unlikely), try for the law firm to be the client.

Do not be intimidated by the retainer that is offered by counsel; it is subject to amendment by either party and counsel is used to discussing various additions, subtractions and other changes to the basic agreement.

But regardless of the origin of the agreement, it is critically important that you make certain that the scope and nature of your assignment is completely and thoroughly spelled out. What, exactly, is expected of you?

- Are you being hired to testify or to consult or both?

- What is your hourly rate? Is it for all work, or is there a different (presumably higher) rate for testimony?

  **Note:** *My rate was constant—the same rate for testimony, for reading depositions, for discussing the case with counsel or with my associates. I believe that is the practice followed by the majority of practitioners, but feel free to consider a different, higher, rate for the testimonial portion of the engagement. Just make sure it is spelled out and counsel is aware of the provision and approves of it.*

- Are you expected to provide data/back-office support? If so, at what rate are your associates to bill?

- Are you expected to produce demonstrative exhibits and/or trial exhibits? If so, at what rate are your associates to bill?

- What, if any, retainer is expected to be maintained and how will it be drawn down? How and when will it be replenished?

- Are you expected to be present for the entirety of a hearing or trial or just your testimony?

- Are you expected to write an expert report? If so, are there limits to the time/billings associated with that report?

- If the matter goes to mediation, are you expected to be present? Are there expectations or limitations regarding the amount of time spent in reviewing the case?

- Are there expectations or limitations regarding the amount of time preparing for testimony?

  **Note:** *Do not underestimate the time necessary to do proper preparation. It may include hours and hours of reading other people's depositions to form your own opinions. It may include reviewing countless number of boxes of documents to come to various conclusions regarding the propriety of actions taken.*

  *The best way to handle this is not to set any specific number of hours to be spent, but to keep counsel fully informed on a frequent basis of the number of hours already spent. In that way, you and counsel can be on the same page regarding billings. Billing surprises are never good surprises.*

- Are you expected to prepare written testimony for yourself or others?

- Are you being hired as an individual, part of a larger organization, or as an LLC?

- What are the billing expectations, i.e., the frequency that you will bill, your billing address, your expectation on the timing of payments?

- Are you going to charge for travel time?

  **Note:** *I never did charge for a travel day, unless I was working on an airplane or working late at night in a hotel room, but others routinely do—so* *think of the trade-off between the extra dollars and the goodwill garnered with an "N/C" on travel days; the decision is yours to make.*

Counsel may balk at the specificity above, and I do understand the reluctance. The point is to try to nail down as many expectations as possible so that there are no surprises later. If it is not to be contained in the Retainer Agreement, I like to have a paper trail, e-mail is fine, regarding some of the points that never made it into the formal agreement.

Get the idea? This is your roadmap to your successful relationship with counsel and client. Do not be intimidated by it. Counsel has seen these issues countless times. Simply be aware that these are the critical issues on which both parties must agree.

## Working with Counsel

The paperwork is done, your relationship is finalized, you are now officially hired to work on *Smith v. Jones* for counsel and the client. What now?

Working with experienced counsel is one of the joys of the profession. As primarily a defense expert, I never ceased to marvel at the depth of understanding that counsel possessed. Quite frankly, the defense bar in the retail securities litigation field is universally deeply experienced and enormously talented. Most any of those counsel could step into an expert role without hesitation, but I suspect that they would generally miss their current role. So, I never hesitate to treat counsel with the utmost respect and admiration. They've earned it.

The first thing to do is to understand and manage the expectations of counsel. Sorry, but you are not equals in this relationship; you work for counsel and the client and therefore must and will take direction from counsel. Yes, you are the expert and counsel is counsel, but make no mistake, counsel will rely on you for the technical aspects and substance of your testimony, but you, at least for now, will defer to counsel on the strategy, the depth, the breadth, the witness list, and the exhibits. Just how much is expected of you must be discussed between you early and often. Just as you tried to capture the depth of your relationship when you fashioned the Retainer Agreement, you must now put those expectations to work in your day-to-day relationship.

It is worth an early phone call to counsel to set these expectations:

### Which documents should you review?

In a major litigation, there will be boxes and boxes of documents (or more recently, huge online data files) will need to be reviewed. Not all of them are relevant to your testimony, and yet, it's tempting to review everything, if for no other reason than to answer on cross-examination that yes, you have reviewed all documents turned over in this matter. But the more substantive reason for review is that you are expected to form opinions based on the evidence, and documents will become evidence. Therefore, the review of all (or mostly all) of the documents produced becomes somewhat of a professional obligation.

But here you run into the reality of economics. Review takes time, time is money, and money is never unlimited. Ask counsel for guidance on exactly what you are expected to review and approximately how much time he or she expects you to spend on document review.

If possible, letting an associate of yours, with a lower

billing rate, review documents is an option. The discussion with counsel regarding document review is critical. I have been witness to too many disputes centering on what counsel considered to be outrageous time spent on document review before any work product is produced.

Remember two things: first, counsel is not the villain—there are no villains; he or she is working with a client who will be reviewing invoices and will undoubtedly be very cost- conscious. Second, if an associate does assist in the review, that name must be proffered to the other side as having worked with you on the case. More on that later.

Be prepared for the reality that some documents take more time than others to review. E-mails may be extensive, but are usually a quick read and contain many redundancies as the e-mail chain is reproduced countless number of times. Many of the e-mails will turn out to be irrelevant, but you must be on the lookout for those that are integral to an opinion that is being formed.

Business records are less repetitive, but take time to understand regarding their context and whether they will be relevant to any opinions you are forming. Manuals and other legal documents must be read carefully and put into context of the other facts set forth in the litigation. Interrogatories and especially depositions and the exhibits attached to the depositions are a black hole of time use.

Very often, depositions are critical to the understanding of the case and may be just as critical to the formation of your opinions, but they take an inordinate amount of time to read, understand, and put into context. Thus, an understanding as to the extent of document review is imperative.

## What do I do when I am reviewing documents?

Once you have the scope of document review settled, you must decide what to do when reviewing them. Do you just read and try to retain the substance of the documents, trusting that your memory will come through amid cross-examination? Should you take notes? On the document? On your computer? Should you send continuous updates to counsel? Can you discuss the documents with your associates? Do you fashion potential exhibits from what you learn from the documents? Can you make an index or a cheat sheet to help in the retrieval process?

All are excellent questions. The answers are largely dependent on counsel's strongly held views, and counsel will have strongly held views, so make sure you check before embarking on a time-consuming document review session. The following are general rules based on my experience:

1.  Notes are permitted, and in fact, for most of us mortals, a review without some sort of memory-jogger is largely a waste of time and money. However, assume that everything you write is discoverable so nothing questionable should be put into writing. The law on this is in flux, and it varies from forum to forum, but you **must** err on the side of caution. If you have any serious concerns, just make a note to discuss with counsel. Far too often, innocent notations become the subject of intense cross-examination which usually leads nowhere, but causes embarrassment, potential loss of credibility, and an opening for additional avenues of examination. This is important enough to warrant being presented as:

**ESSENTIAL RULE NUMBER NINE: Always assume everything you write or otherwise prepare is discoverable and will be seen by opposing counsel. You have been cautioned.**

2. I prefer to highlight in yellow marker on a document (the yellow marking will not reproduce), but to make cryptic notes on a computer file that will allow me to cross- reference to any future items that relate to the initial document. In that way, at least the document I am working from is clean. But remember, if you are asked, your computer file is potentially available to opposing counsel.

3. I do like to keep counsel informed about my findings. The reality is that counsel, or one or more associates, will already be familiar with the documents, so your job is not to inform strictly on the content, but on how it relates to your expertise, how it is assisting you in the formation of opinions, and to suggest exhibits, demonstratives or other work-product materials that might flow from what you have read. Just how to inform counsel and how often to inform counsel is up to the two of you, but generally, I prefer a telephone call to anything in writing. I do have a strong aversion to putting too much in writing. Respecting counsel's valuable time, I try to contact him or her no more often than once a week—until the trial or hearing data approaches when the communication will step up significantly.

4. I will always share my review with the assigned associates in my office, since they are part of my team and are enormously helpful in taking the readings to the next step of exhibit preparation.

Do note, however, that you will be asked on cross-examination the names of all those who assisted you in your testimony and document preparation. Despite opposing counsel's taking careful notes of the names that you proffer, in my experience, nothing has ever followed from that recitation; i.e., none of my associates have ever been called to testify. However, the possibility does exist of a subpoena going out to an associate for corroborating (or contradictory) testimony.

5.   I take notes on possible exhibits from my review of documents. Whether something eventually becomes an exhibit, an opinion, or a component of an opinion will be determined later. But the critical thing is to be thinking when reading, not just trying to get through a boring deposition, but asking yourself: "How does this help?" "How can this information be used?" "Can I relate this information to something else that I have read?" "Does this corroborate or contradict anything else that I have read?"

6.   Finally, I cross index my readings. I try to make sense and put into context everything that is put before me. It is very much like solving a mystery: There may be false leads and irrelevant tracks, but the job of the expert is to fashion opinions based on the evidence—and the written evidence will be in front of you long before the testimony begins. Put it to good use.

## Why am I reviewing these documents?

Look at the big picture and be ready to answer these questions:

- Why have I been given these documents?
- I know I must read them, but why?
- What is expected of me?
- How many exhibits are expected to be produced?
- What are the areas of opinion testimony that counsel sees as relevant?
- What is the timeline for each project?
- What independent research should be done?
- What should be put in writing and what must remain oral between you and counsel?
- Whom among counsel's team should you work with?
- How do I best integrate my industry experience with my new role as an expert witness?

You must assume that there are useful nuggets in everything you read, so read everything with care. From the overview that counsel has given you and the pleadings that counsel has provided, you will have a basic understanding of the issues to be litigated. From that understanding, put the document review into context. For example, if an unlawful margin sellout is alleged, pay attention to anything that has a timestamp or an indication of timing on it. It will be critical to be able to testify as to what happened, when it happened, and the context and consequences that followed. Then, go ahead and construct a tentative timeline that can be added upon and later discussed with counsel. You may be duplicating some work done at the law firm, but in this case, it is a necessary step in the learning process.

• • •

**A Personal Aside:** *The propriety of a margin sellout was the issue in a futures case in Chicago. Timing was everything. Exactly when did the markets crash? Which overseas markets were relevant to a domestic sellout, and when were those markets open for business? When did the accounts became under-margined? When did the firm act? When did the client respond? And when did the markets recover sufficiently to cover the deficit? These were the issues to be resolved before we began discussing the law, rules, and customs and practices in the industry. A well-designed timeline, complex and well-annotated, and suitable for the jury's examination, was a critical part of the case.*

As you might have surmised, I am a great believer in visuals, in exhibits that can tell a story. So, I was always reading documents with an eye to turning the information into an exhibit that will support my opinions. Which comes first? The opinions must come first from a thorough reading of the materials, and only then can exhibits be fashioned. Note, however, that the opinion is far more critical than an exhibit, which only exists to support that opinion.

Therefore, the number of exhibits is irrelevant, since, with or without them, the story will be fully told. But I tend to err on the side of producing more exhibits since, as detailed earlier, visuals are a tremendous way of holding the attention of judges, juries, and everyone in an arbitration hearing room. But do not assume that there is any sort of quota on exhibit production. Your job is to fashion testimony around expert opinions; the exhibits that support those opinions will follow as a matter of discussion between you and counsel. And be aware that even when your exhibits are produced in final form, they can always be jettisoned and remain unintroduced—even after their turnover to opposing counsel.

Project timelines are important to keep a good working relationship between the triumvirate of expert, counsel, and client. The ultimate deadline, of course, is the trial or hearing date, but there are numerous markers along the way. For example, courts will set dates for depositions, discovery cutoffs, and pretrial briefs. Arbitration panels will set discovery cutoffs and FINRA rules mandate that any materials to be used by counsel be turned over to opposing counsel no later than 20 days before the first date of an arbitration. With that in mind, any exhibit must be finalized well before those deadlines. It is possible to use an exhibit that is completed after those deadlines under only three limited circumstances:

First, any document or exhibit can be used on cross-examination of any witness without being turned over to the other side although relevance and other evidentiary matters must still be adhered to.

Second, a chart, graph or table may be used on direct examination without having been turned over to opposing counsel, but it will not be accepted as evidence and therefore will not be considered during the deliberation by the panel. These are known as "demonstrative exhibits" and should be used with caution since not only are they not considered to be evidence, but also, they tend to be admitted, if at all, only following strong objection by opposing counsel and therefore will invariably disrupt the flow of counsel's presentation. In addition, speaking as an arbitrator myself, I have found that there is an inherent prejudice by an arbitration panel in the consideration of these items because, by definition, opposing counsel, for whatever reason, has not been given the opportunity to see and examine them in advance and therefore is at a disadvantage.

My recommendation is to not pick a fight with opposing counsel or the arbitration panel and, if possible, have every exhibit ready to go well before the 20-day exchange period. It is in your client's best interest to do so.

Third, if evidence is discovered after the 20-day exchange period, and it was not possible for it to have been discovered earlier, it is possible to create an exhibit reflecting those new findings, but again, only subject to the acquiescence of the arbitration panel. In that case, counsel will have turned your work over to the other side in the period between the 20-day exchange and the beginning of the arbitration, and an argument will invariably ensue over whether it could have been discovered earlier, and whether opposing counsel has had enough time for a competent evaluation. The panel will decide the admissibility of the document and under what conditions it may be used.

What about doing your own independent research? Well, it might be argued that most of your expertise has been gleaned from your industry experience. But some expertise is presumably derived from your ability to research various aspects relating to that expertise, and then take your expertise an additional step and relate it, and the issue at hand, to the industry as a whole.

In some cases, you might have a team of researchers available to you as in the case of The Bates Group. If that is the case, your job is to help them understand the issues and guide them while they do the fundamental research. Keep in mind, however, that you will be adopting their research, so you must completely understand the parameters, the methodologies, the results, and any shortcomings to defend the resulting work in front of opposing counsel during cross-examination. You must know the research and the resultant exhibits as if they were yours alone.

• • •

**Critical Note:** *I made it a point to heavily footnote all charts, graphs or tables that came out of The Bates Group research arm. Anything that might raise the slightest question was found in a footnote. I would literally take a prospective exhibit, still in draft form, and start asking questions to myself. (I often asked those questions to myself aloud). If the answer was not totally obvious on the face of the document, I would insist on adding a clarifying footnote. In that way, I was anticipating cross-examination questions and the answers to those questions became part of the exhibit itself. When I was finished examining a chart or a graph, it was not unusual to have a dozen or more footnotes on any single exhibit. Undoubtedly, some of the footnotes themselves elicited questions from opposing counsel, but that was a small price to pay to have a flawless document that I understood perfectly.*

In other cases, you must do your own research, which is more difficult than if you had a team behind you, and yet easier to defend since you have created the documentation by yourself. Not everyone, however, has the background or expertise to do research that is professional enough to withstand cross-examination nor to create an exhibit reflecting that research. If you feel that you do not have the research background, or that you do not have sufficient resources available to you to do high- level research, or that you cannot produce trial-quality exhibits, let counsel know, and remember *Essential Rule Number Six*: Never jump or be pushed into an area that is beyond your expertise or capabilities.

There are many solutions to that issue, such as counsel might direct his or her associates to do some legal research that might be useful to you; counsel may hire another expert to testify solely on the research point at issue; or counsel might not consider the point to be of sufficient importance to warrant further discussion. In any case, full disclosure, communication, and discussion with counsel, as usual, is the key.

Regular communication with counsel is extremely important. Early in your relationship, get to know counsel and his or her preferences regarding frequency and method of contact. Most likely, and understandably, counsel would prefer fewer e-mails and more telephone calls. Try hard to adhere to those preferences, but some exchange of draft exhibits, testimony and/or written opinions between you and counsel is inevitable. Just keep in mind the admonition found in Essential Rule Number Nine that everything exchanged is potentially discoverable.

•  •  •

**A Personal Aside:** *A new colleague was having an extremely difficult time defending a matter, so difficult that he wrote to counsel explaining in detail why, in his expert opinion, he could not, in good faith, testify and that counsel should consider settling the matter. He wrote that the defendant, his client, did virtually everything improperly, did not follow his firm's internal guidelines, and the defendant's actions were out of the norm of industry practice. Predictably, counsel went ballistic, not so much because of the substance of the e-mail—counsel already* *knew the weakness in the case—but because his expert's adverse opinion was forever memorialized in an e-mail. Remember Essential Rule Number Nine.*

What is your relationship with counsel's associates? It is critical that you get to know the entire team. Often, lead counsel will be unavailable and being able to call or write co-counsel or an associate of the lead counsel is a valuable asset. Depending on the seniority of the associate, there are times when substantive decisions can be handled by the associate which will give you sufficient direction to keep you focused and working. A good associate is an invaluable tool for counsel, and he or she will rely on the associate for many of the decisions that go into a successful litigation. However, my advice is to keep tabs on decisions made between you and an associate and verify that lead counsel agrees with all decisions made.

**Working with counsel as an expert for the first time; using your experience to good advantage.**

Integrating your former life as an industry professional with your new calling as an expert is your new ultimate challenge in your work with counsel. You have been a great success as a regional, division, or national manager, you have given speeches to hundreds of adoring subordinates, you have introduced new products and services to enhance your clients' welfare, you have made a wonderful living doing what you know best—but those days are now over. You are working in a new role with legal counsel.

To succeed in this new role, take your experience and start applying it to the facts at hand. Always ask:

* In your former position, what would you have done in this situation?

- What would your subordinates have done in this situation?

- What would your former competitors have done in this situation?

- How would a reasonable investor have acted or reacted in this situation?

- Which actors handled the situation at hand perfectly, adequately, inadequately, questionably, or with reckless abandon?

- What rules, regulations, statutes, or customs and practices of the industry may have been violated? (But do not play lawyer and start making conclusory statements or observations. You are not the trier of fact, but an aide to counsel).

Regardless of whom you represent, analyze word by word the pleadings, i.e., the Statement of Claim, the Answer, and any prehearing or pretrial briefs that have been submitted. In effect, you are scrutinizing both counsel's work product. Be impartial, neutral, and extremely inquisitive. When analyzing the pleadings, think along the following lines:

- Which statements in the pleadings seem improbable to you and why?

- If those improbable statements were, in fact, true, what would have been the real-world consequences from an industry or operational standpoint?

- What statements in the pleadings can be verified by documentation?

- Have you seen that documentation?

- Has it been requested by counsel?

- Can you interpret that documentation?

- Are any statements by your counsel patently and objectively untrue or impossible to the extent that an amendment to the pleadings may be necessary?

- Are any claims made by opposing counsel which are so objectively incorrect that a motion to dismiss might be in order?

- Can any statements made by opposing counsel be refuted with documentation?

- Can you refute statements by opposing counsel with testimony based on your experience?

- What exhibits or other documentation would you need to effectively refute opposing counsel's assertions?

- What statues, rules, regulations, manual sections, customs and practices in the industry are in play?

- If there are depositions to be held (or in the case of arbitration, if you had the opportunity to depose), what are the most probative lines of inquiry you would suggest for each of the major players in this matter?

Notes in hand, now go make yourself the expert and confer with counsel. And using your industry experience, go through the pleadings with counsel and enlighten him or her. And yes, your counsel's own work-product should be discussed in the same manner—carefully, as egos may be involved. If you have doubts about statements made in your counsel's work-product, discuss the rationale for the statements. In meeting with counsel, take enough time to be effective and be thoroughly organized. Remember, this may be the first time that your value will be assessed, so be precise and make this meeting the foundation of your future relationship.

Your assistance will continue throughout the discovery period. As each new document is given to you, go through that same analysis:

- What is the industry standard?
- What are the pros and cons of all the relevant players and their actions and reactions?
- How would you or your firm have handled this situation?
- What would have been or could have been an alternative course of action taken by the claimant?
- What does this new document add to the mix of documents already received?
- What documents would you expect to see, but you have not seen?
- Can you interpret for counsel those very technical documents produced by a firm's back office that only an industry expert would understand?
- What actions or reactions are reasonable, given a set of facts that might be contested and have differing interpretations which you, as an expert, might have to interpret in the alternative.

In short, this is your job: to interpret the vast amount of data found in financial services litigation and give to counsel your unique insights garnered through your years of experience. It is an essential rule:

**ESSENTIAL RULE NUMBER TEN:** Understanding and communicating the meaning of words on paper is not makeshift work, but essential to your role. It is your role. This is how you become invaluable to counsel. Giving counsel insights that he or she could not otherwise acquire makes you a unique asset.

### How much should I bill? Finding the perfect balance.

You are working **with** counsel, but you are working **for** a client who is paying your invoices and has two expectations: a professional job and a reasonable price. Unfortunately, both of those expectations are subjective.

Before long, your reputation and your references will assure clients that your work product, and your ability to testify to such work product, will always be first-rate and totally professional. Every day of your professional career you will continue to build on that reputation. And with increasing skill and expertise, there will be no end to the demand for your services.

But clients also need assurance, especially early in your career, that your billings will be reasonable. There are very few open-ended assignments, and almost none on the claimant side of the table. So, while you must read an enormous amount of materials, and expert reports must be written, and time will be spent at the hearing, you must also be sensitive to the client's limitations.

Your billing rate, or rates, have been determined and agreed to in advance; only the number of hours is variable. So, should you maximize those hours? Minimize those hours? Is this a legal, moral or ethical issue? Yes. Legally, you are entitled to be paid for the number of hours you spend on the matter. You and the client are contractually committed.

You, of course, will not cheat and pad the bill. That is not a wink or a nod—but your obligation, pure and simple. If you want to succeed in this business, you will never give counsel or client even a hint that you did not spend the time as billed. But the legal answer is really the easy answer.

What if you need to spend time "getting up to speed," i.e., if there are issues and nuances that perhaps you "should know" as an expert in the field, but long since forgot or are fuzzy on the details since it has been some time since you dealt with that distinction? Is it right, is it ethical, to bill the client for your time researching that which you "should have already known?" The short answer is, *yes*; the more complex answer is *somewhat*. We are, after all, human. We forget the subtleties of complex issues. We may be an expert, but the financial services field is broad and deep. You may be the most qualified person on the planet to opine on a subject and yet you will still have to research, re-familiarize yourself, and bring yourself up to date. To bill for that background refresher is neither immoral nor unethical. Yet, I admit to some hesitation.

Recognizing the human shortcomings and the need to back up and regroup, I will usually take some financial responsibility and either log the time with a "N/A" in the dollar-amount column, or deliberately truncate the number of hours. And I will let counsel and the client know that the reflected time is a percentage of the actual time expended. I do not do this to earn acclaim or gratitude. It is simply a recognition that we share the responsibility for our universal shortcomings of memory and the inability to be perfect. This is clearly my own philosophy, and I suggest that you consider it, but make your own decisions. I will say that when counsel and client realize that the invoice contains what amounts to a discount, there is a touch of gratitude and thankfulness which does not, in the slightest, hurt your ongoing relationship.

What about the time spent sitting in a hearing where you are not an active participant? Should those hours also be truncated? The simple answer is "no." The more complex answer is still "no." You have been invited to be a part of the hearing even when you are not testifying, the opposing expert is not testifying, or even when critical fact witnesses are not testifying. That time spent listening to others will ultimately be reflected in your testimony. Therefore, there is an expectation that you will bill for that time, and you should. There is nothing opaque about this situation.

What about the time spent "debriefing" over drinks or dinner following a day of testimony? Or the time spent back in your hotel room reviewing the day's notes and planning strategy—or just "thinking"? Stop a minute and use some common sense. There is an expectation that there will be long days and nights during a hearing. There is also an expectation that the expert will be an honorable participant in the litigation game. So, what is honorable? Every expert in these situations must make his or her own determination. Accept or discard mine, but understand one absolute: invoicing for every minute spent on the job will not be to your long-term advantage. Your invoice may be paid in full, but it may also be greatly resented. Why would you want to put yourself in that situation?

My philosophy is rather simple although admittedly not standard: during a hearing, I will bill for either an eight-hour day, or a ten-hour day. Even if I begin my day with a strategy breakfast with counsel at 7:00 AM, and end the day writing testimony at 1:00 AM, I will cap my billings at ten hours. If I do not work those extraordinary hours, I will cap the billing at eight hours. Yes, of course, I am leaving money on the table, I could bill more, a lot more, but I look at the hours not billed as a down payment for future assignments with counsel and/or client. Yes, they will notice and they will appreciate it.

Be honest with yourself and you will admit that there are plenty of hours where you are billing but are not productive. It is not your fault, it is simply the way the litigation business is structured. Therefore, to balance that out, I felt comfortable capping my billings.

Recognize that dinner with the "team," even where business is discussed, is not usually terribly productive. I do not bill for that time. The debriefing session where drinks and snacks are taken? I do not bill for that time. It all gets billed as "Participated in arbitration hearing—8 hours."

● ● ●

**Note:** *Your billing statements should always be deliberately vague. Why? Remember Essential Rule Number Nine: "Always assume that everything you write or prepare is discoverable." If your billing memos are ever made part of the evidence, and they certainly might be, and those entries are teeming with specificity, there will be doors opening for opposing counsel to walk through and drill down during your cross-examination: "I see that you billed 2.4 hours on July 15, 2017 to revise Exhibit 44 following a discussion with counsel and branch manager. Let's discuss that conversation in detail for the panel..." Ouch.*

Earlier, I indicated that I did not bill for travel time on the way to a hearing, except when I was specifically working hard on the matter at hand. I never billed on the way home; I preferred to chill out and watch a bad airplane movie, and felt that the client should not have to pay for that. Again, you are entitled to a wholly different viewpoint; I understand that your time is your time and you are away from home no matter what you are doing; I do respect that.

These are just my thoughts; yours may differ and, again, I respect that. Your billing philosophy may be case-specific and client-specific. I only ask that you give serious thought to a general philosophy behind your billings.

**Working with the Client**

Most of your interface as an expert witness in the financial services industry will be with counsel. However, after first speaking with counsel, you will, most likely, also have an interview with the client where counsel is also present, at least telephonically. After all, it is the client who is paying your bills and has everything to gain or lose from the pending litigation. The client has veto power over who is hired as an expert, but in reality, the client leans heavily on counsel's judgment in the technical matter who to hire as an expert witness. Nevertheless, the client will want to speak with you, to inquire of your background, to test your knowledge and your understanding of the facts, and, as unfair as it might seem at this early stage, to elicit preliminary opinions. Do not be surprised if the client even asks you the ultimate questions: "What do you think of our case?" or "What do you think our chances are?"

If counsel wants to hire you, chances are excellent that the client will as well. But your relationship with the client is now just beginning.

How often you will talk to the client will vary greatly.

In some matters, I spoke to the client at the interview stage and then not again until the trial or arbitration. In other matters, there were weekly or even more frequent calls with the client. Sometimes, a rapport developed quickly so that the client would call me directly; other times, all communication would go through counsel.

I do believe that experts working for the claimant or plaintiff will interface with the client more often that those working with a respondent or defendant. The lines of reporting and communication are simpler without a corporate entity in between counsel and expert.

I preferred not to speak with the client without counsel present, usually telephonically, and would urge you to do the same. There are simply too many potential pitfalls, opportunities for misunderstanding, and assignments not coordinated with counsel. All parties will, or should, understand the rationale behind this admonition, and it was rarely a problem for me to insist that we "get counsel on the line" when the client called.

The client is technically your boss. He or she hired you and is paying you for your services. Therefore, it is incumbent upon you to listen carefully to the needs and wants of the client, both in a substantive manner such as ideas on testimonial matters, and in the tangential matters such as scheduling. I will always run the substantive suggestions through counsel; I will try to mention the tangential matters to counsel as well. It can be tricky to serve two masters, the client and counsel, but that is the reality and it must be done. You will be well rewarded to pay attention to the client's wishes.

It is at a hearing or trial that your relationship with the client will undoubtedly blossom. There is an enormous amount of time spent together. There is a reliance factor wherein the client, expressly or not, will acknowlege a dependence on you to assist in a favorable outcome. The client really gets to know you, your personality and your abilities during the process—long before you take the stand to testify. Here, especially in the evening after a day's session, you have the opportunity to spend hours with the client (and counsel) going over new and existing strategy, reviewing the day's events, exchanging opinions, and getting to know one another—even over drinks.

This is the time that professional relationships are made and reinforced. It is valuable both personally and professionally, and I never regretted getting to know the client in that context. This is where repeat business is born; it is an opportunity to grow your business, but it is, of course, grounded not in the social aspect, but in how well you can serve your client as a professional.

# CHAPTER FIVE

# FORMING YOUR OPINIONS

*Writing Your Opinions;*
*Defending Your Opinions*

The expert opinion is the heart of your job as an expert witness in the financial services industry (or any other industry that relies on expert testimony in dispute resolution).

Some opinions, such as those given in federal court, are formalized in a written expert report, with detailed requirements set forth in the Federal Rules of Evidence and the Federal Rules of Civil Procedure. Other opinions are given in the various state courts which may, or may not, follow the federal rules. Still other opinions are simply given verbally in the context of an arbitration or court proceeding.

I urge you to study and internalize Federal Rule of Evidence 702, *Testimony by Expert Witnesses,* which is the authority and justification for your testimony in federal court. I would also urge you to read some commentary which surrounds the adoptions of recent amendments to the rule. The rule states that you may testify in the form of an opinion because of your "specialized knowledge" that "will help the trier of fact to understand the evidence or to determine a fact in issue." It goes on to state that your testimony must be "based on sufficient facts or data" and

Michael D. Weiner

is "the product of reliable principles and methods" and that you have applied those principles and methods "to the facts of the case."

There is an extensive line of court cases which interpret the use of expert testimony. If you are so inclined, I would urge you to read two of them, both readily available online: *Daubert* v. *Merrell Dow Pharmaceuticals, Inc.*, 509 U.S. 579 (1993), and *Kumho Tire Co. v. Carmichael, 119 S.Ct. 1167 (1999)*. In Daubert, the Supreme Court charged trial courts with the role of a "gatekeeper" to limit unreliable expert testimony. The Court laid down five non-exclusive criteria for the admission of expert testimony. The Court in *Kumho Tire* expanded the scope to include non-scientific testimony depending on "the particular circumstances of the particular case at issue." 119 S.Ct. at 1175.

So, you will be testifying, at least in federal court, courtesy of specific, rules which only apply to your testimony. What will it look like? There are rules for that as well. I again urge you to learn and internalize Federal Rule of Civil Procedure 26(a)(2)(B) and the commentary which accompanies the 2010 amendments to Rule 26. That rule does many things, but relevant to your testimony, it sets forth what is required of you when submitting an expert report in federal court. It is worth quoting the rule:

The report must contain:

*(i) a complete statement of all opinions the witness will express and the basis and reasons for them;*

*(ii) the facts or data considered by the witness in forming them;*

*(iii) any exhibits that will be used to summarize or support them;*

*(iv) the witness's qualifications, including a list of all publications authored in the previous 10 years;*

*(v) a list of all other cases in which, during the previous 4 years, the witness testified as an expert at trial or by deposition; and*

*(vi) a statement of the compensation to be paid for the study and testimony in the case.*

Those are the requirements; they are straightforward. When writing an expert report, I do not necessarily follow that order, but I do assure that all the components are accounted for.

•   •   •

**Note:** *The expert report should look professional. It will be received and read by the Court and, of course, by the other side of the case. Although it usually will not become evidence in the lawsuit, it still must be a document that looks worthy of the work that you put into it. It need not be bound, but the typeface should be clean, with about 12-point type, well-margined, and on plain white 8 ½ by 11-inch paper.*

In the first section, entitled "Qualifications," I begin with my name, education after high school, my current position, then an easy-to-read list of previous employments, with dates and a brief reason why that employment is a qualification for this assignment. If your employment history is too lengthy, you can refer the Court to an appendix with your full history, and attach it to the report.

The next section would be entitled "Publications." List all your publications within the last ten years, or state that there are none.

The next section is entitled "Compensation" where I state my hourly rate. There is no need to give a dollar amount to-date.

The next section would be Trial History where you would give full data on previous testimonies or depositions. Although the rule seems to imply that only "trial" or "deposition" testimony is required, I gave, via an exhibit to the report, my full testimony history which included arbitration testimony as well.

I then deviated a bit by putting in a section entitled "Assignment" where I summarized what I was asked to accomplish by counsel.

Penultimately, the essence of the report is a section entitled "Opinions." I combine the requirements of subsections (i), (ii), and (iii) and lay out my opinions, one by one, with headings and sub-headings. I include the specific facts that support those opinions and reference and attach all exhibits that have been prepared to support those opinions. It can, and most likely will, be lengthy, since this is exactly what you will be testifying to, and the reasons why your testimony is probative to the facts at hand. Some of my reports were fifty or more pages, not including the exhibits. I rarely produced a report less than twenty pages. But obviously, size does not matter; content does. Your opinions should be decisive and go to the heart of the matter at hand. Remember your task: To aid the triers of fact in understanding the complexities of the financial services industry and to put the facts at hand into that context.

In addition to your opinions, your reasoning is found there, and your backup to those opinions is fully detailed—whether it was research culled from outside sources or produced internally. This is your only opportunity to formalize and express your opinions. That is a hard-and-fast rule: If a subject matter opinion is not discussed in your report, there will be no expert testimony regarding that matter at trial. Therefore, there is absolutely no reason to try to withhold opinions; you are about to be thoroughly deposed on your report which will include all of your opinions, theories, and rationales.

At the very end of my expert report, I include a section entitled "Reservation" wherein I state that "My opinions are given as of the date below based upon facts known to me as of that date, but I reserve the right to alter, amend or supplement any opinion if there are facts which are brought to my attention at a later date." Frankly, I doubt that there is any legal significance to that section, but it always sounded good to me and gave me a possible escape valve in case there were last-minute facts which might, in fact, alter an opinion.

How much is counsel involved in the preparation of your report? You will want to discuss your opinions with counsel prior to finalization. You may even want to send drafts to counsel now that Federal Rule 26(b)(4)(C) specifically protects those drafts from discovery. But remember two things:

First, the opinions must be yours and yours alone; remember the first characteristic of a successful expert found in Chapter 2: "Be Fiercely Independent." You are the expert; these are your opinions. Of course, they should dovetail with counsel's view of the case and the facts, and your opinions assist counsel in putting forth his or her view of the case. But make sure you are comfortable with any well-meaning suggestions by counsel.

Second, discuss every aspect of your expert report with counsel well before the due date. He or she will not appreciate last minute surprises. Good communication is essential concerning the most important document you will produce that lays the groundwork for your testimony.

Exactly what should be contained in your opinions? How detailed are your opinions and therefore the expert report itself? What qualifies as an opinion?

Your opinions are an outgrowth of your study of the case through documents and depositions. It is not what you might have learned from counsel or your own interviews since those cannot be referenced, but everything else should be referenced through a footnote. This is your opportunity to pull the documentary evidence into your opinions in a linear manner; it is your roadmap to a complete and logical argument. It is also, you might remember, identical to how I treat charts, graphs and tables that are used as evidence during an arbitration: Every nuance and source is cited in a footnote.

That is my style; yours may differ, and that is fine, but let me explain my logic. You are about to be deposed on literally every word contained within the report, and you must defend every word. If you have done the extensive research that is necessary to produce a federal court expert report, then you have an enormous amount of material that you drew upon to create your report.

It does you, and your client, no good to look bewildered when asked in your deposition words to the effect of: "Where did you find evidence for this statement?" or "What is the source for that sentence?" That statement, and virtually every other statement, should have a footnote indicating its derivation. So, assuming I have convinced you that footnoting is an essential part of your Expert Report, I present:

**ESSENTIAL RULE NUMBER ELEVEN:** Everything
in your expert report that can be sourced, should
have a footnote indicating that source. It will make
your life infinitely easier at your deposition and at
trial.

Footnotes can be as simple as: "See Jones Deposition, page
132." But you can also annotate your footnotes and go
further, such as: "See Jones Deposition, page 132 wherein
Mr. Jones denied choking his client, Mr. Johnson, corroborating the testimony of Mr. Smith, his administrative
manager who stated that there was no choking, but rather
aggressive discussions with exaggerated hand gestures as
well as some sort of ethnic dancing. See Smith Deposition,
pages 203-210."

When making any such detailed references, just do
make certain that you are accurately reflecting what the
record states. A footnote is no place for conclusions drawn
from evidence; that is what the main body of your Opinions
section of the Report is for. Rather, a footnote is to reference and to clarify.

But footnotes are also a terrific way to write explanatory
text; items that do not warrant inclusion in the body of the
work, but serve to divulge a minor or collaborative point.
Some of my explanatory footnotes have been known to take
an entire page. The inclusion of the text as a footnote, rather
than in the body of the expert report, is simply indicative
of my belief that it is background, not a necessary part of
the full opinion, but worthy of consideration. It also serves
to more fully disclose my reasoning behind an opinion. A
good lawyer will always look to the footnotes in any brief,
report, or opinion to try to understand not only derivation,
but rationale. Therefore, make certain that your reasoning,

logic and rationales are airtight. And, of course, that same good lawyer is free to depose me (or you) on those footnotes as well as the main body of the report.

If every relevant statement is footnoted, you now have an instant reference point to answer any question which asks for the derivation of a thought or an opinion. In a typical twenty-five-page report (if there is such a thing), I might have more than a hundred footnotes, mostly contained in the "Opinions" section of the report.

How detailed should your opinions be, and therefore how long should your report be? The answer lies in your study of the issues, not in a numeric. You are identifying the critical issues of the case and assisting the trier of facts to come to conclusions. You are an aide to the panel or the judge or the jury. It is not essential that you tackle every single issue in the case. Instead, you must identify those issues which your expertise assists others in making critical determinations. But once you have identified those issues to which you may be of assistance, go to great length in your explanations of your conclusions. You will be cross-examined on your opinions, so it is better to have every nuance written down. Of course, you have just given opposing counsel a much-desired roadmap of your testimony, but you have nothing to hide. You are much better off fully identifying the issues and fully explaining your reasoning in writing, and then feel comfortable defending them on cross-examination.

* * *

**Note, and a Word of Caution:** *As indicated earlier, in federal court, you will not be allowed to testify to anything not contained in your expert report. If attempting to do so,* *opposing counsel will rightly object that he or she has not been given the opportunity to analyze your opinion nor been given an opportunity to depose you on the topic. Therefore, when identifying relevant issues for your Expert Report, understand that there are no second chances to opine on a subject; include the opinion or forever let it be.*

Don't even think about the length of your Expert Report. If there are only a few critical issues, of course your report will be brief. That is perfectly acceptable; there is no award for wordiness. Just make sure that you have footnoted all sources and you have fully explained your rationales (with exhibits if appropriate) and you will be fine.

So, you have created an Expert Report with all the requirements set forth in the federal rules; now you will have to defend it. There are few events in life as particular and precise as what you are about to undergo. Understand clearly that when writing your report, you must always, absolutely, forever keep in mind:

**ESSENTIAL RULE NUMBER TWELVE: Every word of your expert report will be dissected; you must be prepared to be deposed and cross-examined on every word in your report. Therefore, write every word with extreme precision and care. Also, be prepared to defend alternatives, theories, or opinions omitted; they are fair game as well.**

Please take this Essential Rule seriously. You are about to be deposed on the report that you have submitted. If you are in federal court, unless there is an agreement to the contrary, you **will** be deposed. You have given opposing counsel a roadmap to your future testimony; once it is reduced to writing as an expert report, it is difficult to change it. So, assume that you are wedded to your report, and every word that contained therein, through deposition and trial.

The opinions given in an arbitration setting are different. There is (usually) no expert report, only you, the expert, reciting your opinions while the panel writes them down ("the Pencil Test"). Occasionally, by agreement of all parties, a written expert report is mandated in an arbitration. In that case, even though the federal rules are not required to be followed, it makes perfect sense to adhere to them and follow the advice already given. Expect some leniency in evidentiary rulings since you are in a more informal setting, but I tend to treat this situation as if I were in a federal courtroom.

But the usual situation is that there is no written report in an arbitration setting. Refer to Chapter 2, Number 4 where I talk about being clear, organized, and giving a sequential recitation of your opinions. That is still the key to a good presentation, but everything stated about the written expert report also applies to the oral presentation: Choose with care the issues to be presented; know your sources; use your exhibits; choose your words carefully.

By the time of an arbitration hearing, your opinions have been vetted with counsel and you have practiced verbalizing them again and again and again. Perhaps you and counsel have created a dialogue where counsel will prompt you for your next opinion with words such as: "And next, do you have an opinion regarding the applicability of Compliance Manual, Section 4.2.1(a)(ii) to the facts in this matter?" Prompts such as that greatly relieve the pressure to memorize a long list of items. Remember, if you want to bring a "cheat sheet" to the witness table so that you do not forget an opinion about to be offered on direct-examination, you may do so—but it is fair game for opposing counsel to ask to see it before you refer to it. That piece of paper may elicit a new and lengthy line of cross-examination or *voir dire*. It may still be worthwhile to bring it to the table, but keep that caveat in mind.

You have spent a career solving problems and dealing with a myriad of financial-related issues. You are indeed an expert in your field, which means that you may have an opinion on virtually everything that is before counsel when he or she is sifting through the trove of materials received in discovery. Your job, as explained to you, is to opine on the relevant issues, which means that you must disregard those issues that are not relevant. Determining exactly what is relevant is where your communication with counsel is critical.

As necessary as it is, it gives little pleasure to present the obvious as an opinion. Presenting to an arbitration panel that an account gained $1.626 Million over the life of the relationship is obligatory, but tedious. It must be done, but it is not your bread and butter—not what your client is paying you to relate. Why? First, because these days, the mathematics, ins and outs, and therefore the net profit or loss in an account, have been mastered by all experts and even most laymen. There is no longer a great mystery how an account, or a series of accounts, performed. The other side will, most likely, present numbers which are nearly identical to yours. Second, it is not the best use of your talents. An accountant or a well-trained associate who is familiar with basic accounting principles can testify to the narrow area of profit and loss. Your talent, and thus your value, comes from the interpretation of that data.

But if you will be testifying to the "numbers," find ways to make the boring schedules come alive. Those schedules, and the numbers behind them, are a necessary component of any litigation, but are often the catalyst for drowsiness. Knowing that, step up the flair, the drama. Be amazed that the recovery from the downturn took only eight, eight, eight months and after that, the account was in the black! Show the panel that everything except Acme Explosives, Roadrunner Division, made money during the life of the account, and even Acme was long-term positive "If only the client had followed the advice of the broker ("as we heard from Mr. Broker"), and held onto the position." Do not necessarily emphasize or focus on that which is obvious, but do not ignore it because the obvious (in this case, the numerical results of trading) remains a cornerstone of your testimony that will follow.

Therefore, zero in on what supports either the allegations or the defense. What is in the data, the documentation, the testimonial evidence that you can layer upon, you can massage, you can present in a new light that is meaningful to a trier of facts. If, for example, there is an allegation of unsuitability of a unique product, perhaps you can relate the universality of the sales. How many firms were selling this product to how many clients? Were there any articles written about the product? Are the articles meaningful or just puffery? What unique or special need does the product fulfill? How do you know that from your experience? Do you know the creators of the product? Are they available to testify?

If, for example, the allegation is tainted research, if working for the claimants, discover the similarities of all relevant recommendations and determine whether they might fall into a fraudulent pattern. If working for the defense, dig deep into the process and defend that process as industry standard or better.

On the other hand, knowing that only you, as the expert, can give "opinions," there will be issues that are best left for fact witnesses to describe. You can then use those descriptions in your presentation: "As Mr. Wigginstone described, the process of informing his superiors took one day; I agree that it conformed to the XYZ Brokerage Firm Compliance Manual and therefore there is no compliance issue on that point. Furthermore, that is well within the standards of the industry as a whole." In that fashion, the opinion is on the record, you have made your point, but the detailed testimony was left to Mr. Wigginstone who had the first-hand knowledge of the situation.

The goal is to illustrate to the arbitration panel that which they have no ability to discern for themselves. In doing so, your assignment is to make that panel sit up, take notes, and ask questions. I considered my testimony to be less than successful if I could not elicit that kind of interest from an arbitration panel. A secondary goal is to pare down your testimony to those opinions which are unique to an expert with your experience. Offload the more mundane (but necessary) components to relevant fact- witnesses.

* * *

**A Personal Aside:** *In the early days of expert-required arbitrations (all the way back to the 1990s), there was limited use of computer technology, spreadsheet applications, and specialized presentations which, for example, presented month-by-month profit and loss calculations which neutralized the additions and withdrawals from an account. There* *were, therefore, pitched battles over "the numbers." The issues were very often centered on those differing numbers and how the facts in the case fit into the arithmetic story. Those days are gone; today, even the most unsophisticated expert has the expertise, or can hire the expertise, to give an accurate picture of the mathematics and can create an acceptable presentation to an arbitration panel. But freeing up experts to concentrate on issues other than mathematics allowed for more sophisticated expert presentations, sometimes on point, sometimes not.*

## Omitting Your Opinions or the "No-Opinion" Opinion

There is one sensitive area worthy of consideration. In rare occasions you, counsel, or both of you may determine that your opinions and your testimony will not be useful or necessary and you are stricken from the witness list. This usually occurs at the very last minute, sometimes minutes before you are scheduled to take the stand. Consider this to be tactical and no reflection on you or your work.

Generally, this situation occurs for one of two reasons, both of which reflect the risk/reward calculation of a witness subject to cross-examination: First, the determination that the risk of negative testimony being adduced on cross-examination is too great vis à vis the potential benefits derived from the opinions offered on direct examination; or, second, that the litigation is going so well that there is no need for additional testimony, even expert testimony, given even a remote possibility of adverse testimony being garnered on cross-examination.

In the first instance, you or counsel might conclude that, given the substance of your pending opinions, there is too little that will be proffered to make the risk of cross-examination worthwhile; i.e., "Thanks, but I don't think so—the risk is too great given what we have to offer." In the second instance, it is more along the lines of "We believe that things are going so well that it is not necessary for you to testify. Thank you for your time and effort."

The client must be consulted, and will be consulted, prior to your testimony being pulled. It is likely that he or she is unable to fully comprehend the risk/reward matrix, and that must be explained in the heat of the moment. Remember, the client has already paid for your testimony preparation, and might be understandably alarmed to see it go unused—both from a financial and a substantive point of view. Generally, it is up to counsel to make sure that the client is comfortable with the decision and can see the benefit of "less is more."

\* \* \*

**A Personal Aside:** *The last-minute cancelation of my testimony has happened to me on more than one occasion, including several important federal trials, and I admit to have had very mixed feelings. On the one hand, experts must do what is best for the client and if counsel feels that "no testimony" is better than "testimony," one must accept that decision. On the other hand, testimony was my career and my livelihood. I was prepared to testify, I had spent hours preparing, cross-examination did not phase me, and clearly being pulled at the last moment was a huge letdown.*

On more than one occasion, I was the one who first suggested that I not testify. Those instances were particularly delicate in that I had to initiate the discussion with both counsel and client and have clear and persuasive reasons for my suggestion.

Being pulled from the lineup is a fact of professional life (professional athletes encounter it all the time). To pull an expert witness, and his or her opinions, is a judgement call that is grounded on the particular situation and the unique circumstances. Sometimes, in retrospect, the decision was correct, other times, not so much. But then, unfortunately, we never do have the luxury of hindsight.

CHAPTER SIX

# Now Comes Your Deposition

## *The Five Keys*

To give an effective deposition, you must understand what a deposition is all about: It is an exploratory operation. Dr. Opposing Counsel is there to investigate, to search, to probe, to learn. Forget your preconceptions about depositions being harrowing experiences where tempers fly and voices are raised. Although that is not unheard of, far more often the tone is muted and the pace is slow for a good reason: The fireworks, if any, will fly at the trial—this is a fact-finding mission. Counsel is gathering intelligence from you. Your job is to be honest, answer the questions, parse your answers, and let the questioner do the bulk of the work. I have spoken to many first-time deponents who were fearful not of the topic nor the subject matter or case knowledge, but of the impending tone and tenor of the deposition. That fear always proved to be unfounded.

Muted and slow, however, is not an invitation to relax. Although it may appear to be a low-key event, it is not. Your words (and sometimes your face) are being recorded for two reasons: To gather information that will be used at trial; and to have the evidentiary backup that can be used against you if your trial and deposition testimony differ.

You are somewhat on your own. Your counsel will be there and will undoubtedly be making objections, but there is no judge to rule on the objections—the objections are made to preserve a record. You will be instructed to answer the questions even if an objection has been entered. Occasionally, however, your counsel may instruct you to not answer the question. If that is the case, do not answer; let the lawyers fight it out—you will never be in legal jeopardy by following direction given by counsel. But in general, you will be answering virtually all opposing counsel's questions as if it were a quieter, more wide ranging, more unfocused cross-examination. It is.

The setup is simple. Your deposition will be held in a non-judicial setting, typically in a conference room in the offices of one of the attorneys. There will be a court reporter present to take down everything that is said in the deposition, and sometimes a videographer as well. In addition to opposing counsel, he or she might bring associates and/or paralegals. Do not be surprised, and do not be put off, to see the opposing client or a representative of the client in the room as well. This can be distracting, but you must put all distractions out of your mind. You will be accompanied by your counsel, perhaps an associate of counsel, but usually no one else. If you need any moral support, plan on getting it from counsel.

Upon entering, introductions and handshakes will occur, perhaps some small talk will take place, refreshments offered, and then you will be sworn in by the court reporter. From that point on, a record is being made which will become a permanent part of the proceedings. Every word, every aside, and, if videotaped, even every gesture will be recorded—so do be aware that you are in a formal, official setting despite the non-judicial appearance. The fact that you are sworn means that you are under oath to tell the truth; do not take that lightly—there are penalties for perjury.

Opposing counsel (who will be questioning you) will open by giving you a set of basic instructions. Those instructions might include a direction to wait until the question is finished before answering, to feel free to ask for a break, to answer orally without a nod or head shake, whether you are on any medications which would prevent you from answering questions fully and truthfully, and so forth. You will be asked if you brought the items requested in a *subpoena duces tecum*, the formal request for documents. Your counsel will invariably jump in here to answer that question. If he or she does not, simply answer to the best of your ability. There will be exhibit books available for your reference, and perhaps some loose documents that you may or may not have seen before. Put all documents aside, including that which you brought to the deposition, until directed to look at any one particular document.

Your first key is to relax. It will do no one any good if you are overly nervous to the point of blanking on answers that you do, or should, know. Remember the first tip for an effective cross-examination? It was to relax. That applies here as well. So, take that deep breath, recognize that you are indeed the expert whose opinions are your own and perfectly defensible, and let the questions proceed.

Your second key is **not** to be relaxed. What? Right; relax, but never forget that this is deadly serious, that every word will be scrutinized and despite all efforts to be informal, friendly, and personable, the person across the table is not your friend. He or she is there to represent a client who is averse to your client. As I mentioned above, opposing counsel will prove that it is not necessary to be hostile to be an effective opponent—never let down your guard; think before you speak just as you would do at trial on cross-examination.

* * *

**A Personal Aside:** *It is hard to be anything but relaxed when you have known opposing counsel for 30 years, have broken bread with him, and consider him to be a friend and a colleague. The temptation in that deposition was to dialogue, to say stupid things like: "We both know better than that" or "Come on; let's be serious." But, of course, that would be devastatingly unfair to my client and would put my personal relationship ahead of my professional obligations. So, I resisted, did the deposition as if I knew not the opposing attorney, and only later, did we have a drink.*

Your third key is to be prepared. You will be relaxed if you are as prepared for your deposition as you will be for trial since you are about to be tested on all aspects of the case, but especially regarding your opinions and the derivation of those opinions. If your involvement included a review of all documentation, you must be familiar with all such documents when counsel directs you to them and begins asking questions about them. It is perfectly fine to ask for time to re-familiarize yourself with any document; a deposition is not a memory test and you have every right to see and digest any document before answering a question regarding that document.

I never downplay the importance of preparation for a deposition; it can be intense and very time consuming. It can take you many, many hours to gain the confidence that you know the documentation, depositions of others, your opinions, and the derivation of your opinions. But if you have thoroughly done your homework, you will enter the deposition with confidence and will do beautifully.

Note that your counsel can, and will, assist you in deposition preparation. You will undoubtedly spend many hours going over the case materials with counsel, anticipating the lines of questioning and simply getting ready for the examination. If, for some reason, counsel seems unworried or uninterested about your forthcoming ordeal, be pro-active and request some time with him or her; it is worth it to the client (despite some possible carping over your invoice) to have you both prepared and comfortable.

The fourth key is to make opposing counsel do the bulk of the work. This means that you must never volunteer gratuitous information. Gratuitous information is exactly what counsel is hoping for. Remember, unlike a trial, depositions are expected to be somewhat of a fishing expedition, so opposing counsel will be extremely interested in any "fill in the blank" answers that you might volunteer. If a question asks for X, give counsel X, not "X, but if you include Y, then it would be XY." If you feel that you cannot answer a question without misleading counsel, ask that the question be rephrased. That is perfectly acceptable, although it may begin a dialogue as to why you were unable to answer the question as first posed.

Furthermore, never guess at an answer. Do not try to please opposing counsel with an answer of which you are unsure. Never assume that by simply answering a question you are that much closer to the exit door. An answer that is the result of a guess, educated or not, is simply an invitation for additional questions. Instead, rather than offering such a guess, if your answer has roots in documentation, ask to see any relevant documents. It is your duty to answer all questions accurately, and if more documents are the key to accuracy, you are entitled to see them. If your answer is rooted in your expert report, ask to refer to the report before answering the question.

There will undoubtedly be many open-ended questions encouraging you to "fill in the blanks." Those questions simply represent good deposition technique, albeit terrible trial technique. (Depositions are for fishing, trials are for sharpshooting.) Answer open-ended questions to the best of your ability, knowing that at trial, if you give a more expansive answer to the same question, you will undoubtedly be asked why you did not include those segments in your deposition.

Conversely, if you give a more restrictive answer at trial, you may very well be asked why your answer is narrower, and if you are intending to drop the omitted points which were contained in your deposition testimony. It may seem that you cannot win, but no one is perfect or has perfect recall, and those trial questions are certainly not fatal.

Do not mislead, do not stretch the truth, do not be cute, but also do not volunteer any information. This is not direct examination where you are dying to tell your story; this is a deposition where opposing counsel is gathering information and ammunition.

The final key is to be mature: do not argue; do not be combative; do not be sarcastic or condescending. Do not play lawyer and try to anticipate questions or think you know where counsel is going. Just answer the questions that are put to you to the best of your ability.

In December of 2000, Rule 30(d)(1) of the Federal Rules of Civil Procedure was amended to put a 1 day, 7-hour time limit on any federal court deposition—barring unusual circumstances which would allow for additional testimony to be taken. An extension of the 7-hour limit will now be granted only by court order or by stipulation of the parties. From the perspective of a deponent, the amendment is a welcome change from the previous standard which allowed federal courts to adopt local rules modifying the 7-hour limit.

But trust me, seven hours in a deposition is a very long day. Do your best to focus, to pace yourself, and be mindful and reconciled to the fact that you are not in control of the proceeding. Opposing counsel will continue the formal dialogue until he or she is satisfied that there are no further questions to be answered or the clock strikes 7 hours.

If you are being deposed in a federal court case, the usual situation, opposing counsel will be asking you questions that are largely based upon your expert report. Remember, you have conveniently given counsel a roadmap of exactly what needs to be discussed, and therefore, it shall be done.

He or she will most likely begin with your qualifications, your education, and your background. This is done for two primary reasons: First, your background is, presumably, a softball topic, and you will be set at ease in answering those questions. Putting you at ease is good for opposing counsel to get all possible information from you not only on this background information, but on the substantive questions that will follow.

Second, counsel wants to discover if there are any glaring deficiencies or contradictions in your C.V. This is an important topic for counsel for impeachment purposes (the contradictions), and also if counsel believes that there may be potential qualification issues (the deficiencies). Remember that under recent Supreme Court rulings, being qualified as an expert is no longer a *pro forma* exercise. The *Daubert* and *Kuhmo Tire* decisions made it clear that expert witness testimony must adhere to certain professional standards, and counsel will be probing your qualifications that form the basis for allowable testimony in the litigation at hand. There may very well be a "Daubert hearing" on your qualifications, so assure that your C.V. is accurate and complete and the oral answers to any questions concerning your background are likewise accurate and complete.

The questions will then most likely move to your report, focusing on your opinions and the documentation you used as source material for those opinions. As indicated earlier, every word in your report is important and fortunately you will have written the report with this deposition in mind. The questions will be detailed, and do not be surprised if counsel goes line by line, word for word, and your deposition might last until the 7 hour limit is invoked.

You must be able to defend the words on the page, but equally important, you must be able to defend the choices that you made in issuing your opinions, the validity of your logic in connecting your opinions to the source material, and what you did **not** include as part of your report, and why. A good attorney can and will shift the focus from the words that you have written to why certain items or theories were not included. In that way, a more complete picture of your preparation, philosophy, and your thought process will be examined.

For example, if you cite one particular treatise in defense of a position, counsel may ask if you have read three or four others, pulling copies from a briefcase, and then extensively citing from those papers, asking for your reaction vis à vis your stated opinions and the facts of the matter before you. Or, if you have graphed a particular aspect of the data, counsel may ask why you omitted, or failed to highlight, certain other aspects, presumably more favorable to his or her client. Or, if you have cited a provision in a manual, counsel may refer you to other citations hoping to cast doubt on your conclusions.

The best-case scenario is that you are prepared for these encounters and have solid reasons why any alternatives were not included. But if you are not so prepared, simply answer that you did not consider the alternative offerings, or that you were unaware of its existence. It may not be the most comfortable answer, but it is the most truthful. A side-benefit is that now you have a roadmap of where opposing counsel may go during your trial examination, and you can be better prepared.

You will also be quizzed on the report of the opposing expert. This is not an opportunity to be negative in a gratuitous manner, but you will undoubtedly have professional differences with that expert and his or her report. You must be prepared to speak to those differences and most importantly, why you feel that the data, the assumptions, the logic, the methodology and/or the conclusions are incorrect. Yes, you will be giving up information that you would rather hold back and only give that information in the form of a dramatic surprise at the trial, but trials do not (generally) work that way—that's why they call this process "discovery." Thus, it is your responsibility, and opportunity, to provide a full and accurate critique of the opposing expert's work product.

When opposing counsel is satisfied that there is nothing further that can be wrung out of you, he or she will indicate that there are no further questions. Don't relax quite yet. Your counsel will then have an opportunity to ask questions on topics you had already covered. Such a "direct" examination may be necessary on issues that counsel feels that you may have left the wrong impression, or that a particular answer should have a broader explanation. But this is not a trial, this is not true direct examination, so expect very few, if any, clean up questions.

A final word: if there is more than one opposing party, there will be multiple attorneys in the room, each representing his or her own client. Each counsel has the right and the opportunity to ask questions of you; this is often where multi-day depositions take root. There is little you can do about it. If things get too repetitious, your counsel will object, but again, following the objection, you must bite your upper lip and carry on. But do be aware that fatigue is a real issue; if you get too tired, make sure your counsel is aware of it and the parties may agree to stop and reschedule the remainder of the deposition for another time.

●  ●  ●

**A Personal Aside:** *The lengthiest deposition I was subjected to lasted three full days where I was questioned by three senior attorneys (with a plethora of onlookers) representing three different governmental agencies. I wish I could say it was repetitive, but the questioning was based on three different (and relevant) federal statutes, each with its own take on how that law applied to the facts in the litigation. It, therefore, gave me no real reason to complain.*

What becomes of your deposition? First, of course, opposing counsel and a bevy of associates will dissect your every word and use their yellow highlighters to focus on answers that might prove useful in their impending cross-examination of you. As mentioned earlier, one of your trial-preparation jobs is to study with extreme care your own deposition and to anticipate the yellow highlights of opposing counsel.

When reviewing your own deposition, try to see it from the eyes of opposing counsel. What statements might give them a line of questioning that you might not have contemplated? What was stated somewhat inarticulately? What would you like to change if you had the chance, but might now be picked up by opposing counsel as a line of questioning? What did you say that was simply incorrect and not picked up by you or by your counsel? If you spend the time to read your deposition with those eyes, your later cross-examination will go that much smoother.

Second, as it was once said (in so many words), and continues to be true (absolutely):

"Anything you [write] can and will be used against you in a court of law if, at trial, you contradict a statement made during your deposition."

In that case, you will be confronted by opposing counsel in a manner such as the following:

> Q: "Mr. Very-Confused, do you recall giving a deposition on July 4, 2004 wherein, on page 194, you stated the following: 'Frankly, since I have never understood the meaning or the significance of that table of numbers; I never considered it important to my opinions.'"
>
> A: "Yes, sir, I do recall that."

Q: *"And yet today, in your direct testimony, in reference to that table, those very same numbers, did you not state the following: "That table of numbers is the primary source of my expert opinion that the account of the client was handled in an illegal and immoral manner."*

A: *"Ah, I guess that is correct...May I have a break, please?"*

Q: *"So which is it: the numbers were never considered as a source of your opinion since you never understood them, or they are at the heart of the opinion?"*

A: *"Maybe I understood the numbers but not the table?"*

Q: *"Really, Mr. Very-Confused?"*

A: *"May I speak with counsel, please?"*

Q: *"No, I would like an answer to the following question: 'If you never understood the numbers in the table, how can the very same table of numbers be at the heart of your opinion?'"*

A: *"I really need a break."*

Q: *"Absolutely. I have no further questions of this useless witness."*

Of course, the dialogue at the trial wherein you are defending a deposition will not be as dramatic or as extreme. Undoubtedly, the differences are significantly smaller and are explainable—in which case you should take every opportunity to explain fully. But the point is: Do not give opposing counsel the slightest opportunity to question differing testimony; try to reduce to zero the daylight between your testimony in your deposition and your trial testimony. To do so, you must be rock solid on your deposition testimony and make sure it conforms completely with the testimony you will be giving at trial.

# CHAPTER SEVEN

# VENUES

## The Arbitration Room

A little background: In the financial services industry, most disputes are settled through the arbitration process. This is a product of an industry push in the 1980s to make the arbitration process mandatory in order to avoid the costs and lengthy time- frames of commercial litigation found in the federal court system. In 1987, the industry got what it sought in a Supreme Court case, *Shearson/American Express v. McMahon*, which determined that the holding of a 1953 Supreme Court case, *Wilko v. Swan*, prohibiting mandatory arbitration under the Securities Act of 1933 was inapplicable to the Securities Exchange Act of 1934. Since most private arbitrations are filed with reference to the anti-fraud provisions of the 1934 Act, *McMahon* greatly expanded the use of arbitration in securities disputes and at the same time, made the use of arbitration a more acceptable method of dispute resolution.

It did not take long for virtually every securities firm on "the street" to adopt language in its customer agreement that mandated that any dispute be held before an arbitration forum. That forum was usually FINRA (then the National Association of Securities Dealers, the "NASD"), but occasionally through private dispute resolution firms such as JAMS (Judicial Arbitration and Mediation Services) or AAA (American Arbitration Association). In effect, if a customer wished to participate in the securities markets, and if that customer did not expressly delete the arbitration clause (and get acquiescence to that deletion), the customer has waived his or her right to go to court. Clearly, it was, and is, only the savvy, usually the institutional customer, that has the knowledge and the clout to have the arbitration clause deleted.

The practical result is that if a securities dispute is ever filed in the court system, the securities firm will simply ask the court for removal of the matter to the chosen arbitration forum based upon a signed contract between the parties, noting that the substance of said contract was affirmed by the Supreme Court. In every case of which I am aware, the court acquiesced to the removal and the parties resolved the dispute in arbitration.

The NASD soon expanded its arbitration processes and mechanisms, as did the individual securities exchanges, notably the New York Stock Exchange and the American Stock Exchange, followed by regional stock exchanges such as the Pacific Stock Exchange and the Boston Stock Exchange (both now defunct). Today, FINRA, the successor organization to the NASD which also took over the New York Stock Exchange arbitration forum, is the primary arbiter forum for securities disputes.

Ask most attorneys who practice securities law, at least those who represent securities firms, and if you catch them in a forthright mood, they may admit that the arbitration process is no longer quicker, cheaper, more reliable than the courts, or even the preferred forum. It just might be a case of "Be careful what you wish for:"

- There is no precedential value in an arbitration decision which frustrates experienced litigators who are used to relying on precedent to argue the finer points of law.

- The length of an average hearing has greatly expanded rivaling that, or even exceeding, that of the courts.

- The time required to bring a case to an arbitration forum is also lengthy, especially during periods of market crises where the volume of disputes grow geometrically.

- The lengthy hearing process drives up the cost of dispute resolution, essentially voiding one of the primary reasons for wishing to replace the court system with the arbitration system.

- Decisions will usually take no less than a month to be delivered to counsel instead of an immediate response from a jury or a judge.

- While there is some delineated discovery, in most arbitrations there are no depositions which greatly frustrates the cross-examination process and the careful planning which would otherwise occur.

- The rules of evidence, be they federal or state, do not apply, leaving the admission of evidence to the discretion of the arbitration chair. This often results in rulings which appear to be arbitrary, or at least inconsistent, which again greatly frustrates seasoned trial attorneys.

- In most cases, there are no written opinions issued by an arbitration panel, simply a monetary award (if the claimant is successful), which

leaves the parties wondering how the panelists
derived the awarded amount, and leaving a void
as the reasoning behind the award.

But whether counsel likes it or not, your matter is now in
arbitration. There are no further delays, the twenty-day
exchange of documents has been accomplished, you have
formulated your opinions, you have met with counsel, your
direct examination is ready to go, your exhibits have been
exchanged with the other side, you have given to counsel
your best analysis of and rebuttal to the opposing expert's
report or work-product, you are dressed to kill. Let's go
into the room.

An arbitration room is not particularly awe-inspiring. It
is a conference room whether in a hotel, a business center,
FINRA offices, or even a law firm. There are no judicial
trappings, no raised daises, no flags, no sergeant-at-arms or
bailiffs. There may be a court reporter if one or both sides
prefer to see transcriptions of testimony either in real-time,
in a rough draft form in the evening, or later in the process.
It is simply a venue where serious discussion of important
issues will be heard.

The three arbitrators will be seated at the front of the
room with the court reporter, if there is one, off to the side
where he or she can best hear and transcribe all witnesses.

In general, each side of the dispute will take one side
of a U-shaped table arrangement. As an expert, my seating preference is to hide—not literally, but largely for the
previously stated reason of independence-appearance. Thus,
I prefer to take an inconspicuous place at the very end of
the lineup, or even in a chair near the back of the room.
The only exception is when the opposing expert or experts

are testifying; I like to be close to counsel to better communicate my thoughts.

The proceeding will begin with a script provided by FINRA or by the alternative forum. It is boilerplate; no need to get your radar off of standby just yet.

After the script is read and acknowledged, the chair will then ask if both (or all) parties accept the composition of the panel. This is usually routine, although I have been in multiple hearings where the impartiality of one or more arbitrators was called into question. This event is unusual since, unless it is newly discovered evidence, there generally had been months gone by to make any challenge through the FINRA arbitration process.

Assuming the composition of the panel is accepted, the chair will then ask for introductions of everyone in the room, including those who have been admitted, or hope to be admitted, as onlookers. It is quite unusual for a non-party (except a corporate representative) to be allowed to observe; there must be good cause shown and one or more counsel will generally object. If such an objection is entered, the panel will be forced to rule on the request for a non-party to stay in the room. However, you, as an expert witness, are, by FINRA rule, allowed to stay and observe all testimony.

The most controversial request will be for the broker to be allowed to stay in the room to hear the testimony of his former client, the claimant. If the broker is a named party to the action, there is no question that he or she may stay in the room for the entire proceeding. In fact, it is considered extremely bad form for any named party **not** to be present for the entirety of the hearing. But if the broker is not a named party, done for strategic reasons including the exclusion of the broker from the hearing room during all testimony but his or her own, then claimant's counsel will invariably object to the presence of the broker. Panels, in my experience, will usually recuse the broker from hearing any testimony, including opening statements (which are technically, not considered to be evidence).

Usually, but not always, counsel will introduce everyone on his or her side of the table. You will be introduced by name, affiliation, and noted as an expert witness. If counsel asks that you introduce yourself, do the same: name, affiliation, and "expert witness for [X]." Note that if there is more than one party, and if you are representing only one of the parties, make it clear that you are representing just that party. Obviously, if you have been hired by multiple parties, that should be made clear as well.

The chair will then note that the panel has read and reviewed what is usually known as "Arbitrators' Exhibit One" which consists of the pleadings, any motions, and if applicable, any briefs filed by the parties. If there are any unresolved motions, the chair will either give a ruling, defer the ruling, or ask for arguments on the motions. None of that is of great concern for you, the expert witness; life goes on without your input.

Upon resolution of the outstanding motions, the chair will usually then ask if there are any other outstanding issues to be resolved before testimony begins. This is either routine; i.e., "Nothing, Mr./Ms. Chair," or it is far from routine: a slew of accusations regarding alleged discovery violations, witnesses who need subpoenas, exhibits not turned over in a timely manner, witnesses who need sequestration, missing documents, requests for sanctions, and so on. The panel will resolve every one of these issues before testimony can proceed, or, in some cases, can defer a decision until the end of the hearing.

Opening statements will come next; claimant(s) first, respondent(s) next. Whatever formality there is in the arbitration world takes place front and center as counsel (usually) rises, as if in court, and proceeds to give what is supposed to be a summary of what he or she intends to prove. There is not supposed to be argument, just summary of the proposed evidence to be checked off at the end of the hearing, during closing arguments, as "proven" through testimony or documentary evidence. Most opening statements are about fifteen to thirty minutes in length, but obviously, they can vary substantially in length.

The most effective opening statements are just that: a summary. But some counsel stray, make legal arguments, make factual assumptions, and in many cases, go on far, far too long.

*       *       *

**A Personal Aside:** *I participated in a hearing where opposing counsel, a very experienced trial lawyer, told the panel that he would be taking a minimum of two and a half hours, perhaps more, to make his opening statement which was replete with animated PowerPoint slides, photographs, screen captures, summaries of proposed exhibits, and legal decisions. When the panel protested, he stood firm, offering the panel the ultimate threat: "I will consider that I was not given a 'full and fair hearing and an opportunity to be heard' unless you allow me my full opening statement." (That threat is real; each counsel is asked at the conclusion of a hearing whether he or she had been given a "full and fair hearing and an opportunity to be heard." A negative answer is cause for great alarm* *back at FINRA Central, and because there may be adverse consequences, arbitrators hate to be the subject of disgruntled counsel). The opening statement went on for almost three hours—to the acute displeasure of many in the room.*

Do listen carefully to the other side's opening statement. It is designed to be a roadmap of what will be proven. From the expert viewpoint, I take careful notes of those areas in which I believe the opposing expert will be offering testimony. It is an educated guess because you have, presumably, already been provided with exhibits from the opposing expert in the 20-day exchange. Morph, in your mind, those exhibits with what opposing counsel is saying. Try to determine whether the exhibits that you have seen dovetails with counsel's recitation. Counsel will be very interested in your observations on proposed expert testimony vis à vis the conclusions contained in the actual expert documents received. This will undoubtedly be the first in-hearing opportunity you will have to contribute in a substantive manner to the outcome of the hearing.

Next, respondent's counsel will give an opening statement. Listen carefully here as well; your role, if you are on defense, will be described. There should be no surprises regarding your proposed testimony since you have worked with counsel to define your role and your testimony. If there is some, any, discrepancy, make a note and at the first reasonable opportunity, discuss it with counsel. (As indicated earlier, it may be easier to approach an associate during these most hectic and critical of times).

And now the testimony begins. The claimant's counsel will call the first witness who will take an appropriate seat. Appropriate, in this context, means basically wherever the court reporter can best hear him or her or, if there is no reporter, either next to his or her own counsel, or perhaps in the center of the U-shaped table. In other words, there are no real rules, just convenience.

The one formality reflecting the solemnity of the occasion, similar to a matter in court, is the swearing in of all witnesses. The chair or the court reporter will ask the witness to rise, raise his or her right hand and ask if the witness does swear (or affirm) to tell the truth, the whole truth, and nothing but the truth. With that bit of pomp, the questioning now begins.

There is an ongoing debate as to the most effective order of witnesses. In a retail securities matter, very often counsel for the claimant will call the client's contact, the broker, as the first witness. The purpose of having the broker testify as the first witness is, presumably, to allow the claimant, who is in the room, to hear the broker's side of the story, i.e., the defense. Thus, when it is the client's turn to testify, he or she can directly answer the assertions made by the broker.

The broker will be examined as an "adverse witness" which allows counsel to ask leading questions (prohibited under strict rules of evidence for a witness on direct examination) and treat the witness as legally "hostile." Thus, even though the strict rules of evidence do not apply in an arbitration proceeding, this is one exception invariably adhered to; the broker can be treated as a hostile witness on direct examination.

Another school of thought is that claimant's counsel should call the claimant first, establishing the claims with, presumably, the strongest witness who is closest to the facts at issue. Of course, this reverses the ability to rebut. It is now the client who has told his or her story and the broker can rebut that version. Recall that the broker was, in this scenario, not in the room to hear the testimony of the client. Counsel may wish to call the broker immediately after the client has testified, this depriving the broker a chance to digest the client's testimony second-hand—through discussions with counsel or even a transcript. Tactics, tactics, tactics.

These are tactics without a resolution as to which is "best." From the expert point of view, it really does not matter who goes first, second or last. Your job remains the same: formulate opinions through both documentary and oral evidence and express those opinions through your testimony.

* * *

**A Personal Aside:** *In one remarkable hearing, counsel for the claimant surprised everyone in the room and called me, the expert witness for the respondents, to the stand as his first witness. Calling the expert for the other side is almost unheard of; calling him as the first witness is all but unprecedented. After a great deal of heated discussion, I was allowed to testify as an "adverse witness" under rigid set of conditions, e.g., no ad hominum questions, and the acceptance of all my exhibits as mathematically correct.*

Direct testimony will be immediately followed by cross-examination of that same witness which, as indicated earlier is usually longer than direct, as counsel probes the assertions made on the direct examination. Counsel will use the same documents used with the witness on direct, but he or she can, and will, also introduce different exhibits (albeit previously exchanged) to elicit a different slant on the issues.

In fact, as also indicated earlier, there may be documents that were never exchanged between counsel until the very moment that the witness is presented them. Assuming no authentication issues, that is accepted practice and procedure on cross-examination.

On and on the witnesses come and go. The panel makes notes, rules on objections, admits evidence, occasionally denies the admission of an exhibit, asks an occasional question, but largely remains silent. Are they forming any opinions as the hearing proceeds? Of course; they are human and are swayed by things like credibility, demeanor, and yes, even facts. And even though FINRA's Arbitrators Manual states that arbitrators should not discuss the case among themselves during the course of a lengthy hearing, a badly kept secret is that yes, of course they do. They discuss the hearing and their impressions at every break and at every meal. But arbitrators are honorable public servants and evidence is cumulative, so while there may be discussions, there generally will not be conclusions drawn until it is time to deliberate.

By the time the hearing is underway, you have already formulated your opinions; you have reduced them to outline form that your counsel will lead you through. Why then are you in the room listening to testimony? Is that not both irrelevant and unnecessary? No and no.

You are in the room on day number one because you play a critical role in counsel's presentation of evidence. You have a particular expertise that filters both lay and expert testimony in a unique fashion—that is why, in many cases, your presence is requested from the beginning of the arbitration until the very end. And you put that expertise into play by listening with a finely tuned ear, taking notes of testimony from fact witnesses, and giving counsel your insights based on your experience. There is very good reason for you to be in the room for lay testimony: To add your perspective to the total mix of information. That perspective, derived from your experience and the unique filter that you possess, is what counsel will demand of you and what the client will be eager to explore with you.

There will be numerous times that oral testimony from fact witnesses will affect your carefully laid opinions. Hopefully, you will hear evidence that bolsters your opinions—and the use of fact-witness testimony to strengthen your opinions is extraordinarily effective. It brings the matter home to that day, that witness's testimony, that line in the transcript. If you can reference another witness's testimony to reinforce your opinions, do so without hesitation.

Can the testimony of another witness actually change your carefully formulated opinions? Absolutely. But fear not; you have time to rethink those opinions, to modify them, to omit them, or even to add to them. If you are on defense, you will likely be the last witness to testify, so that you have the luxury of staying up all night, or several nights, before your testimony to assure that your anticipated testimony is still complete, accurate, and relevant. If you are testifying for the claimant, there is less time to make revisions (since you will be testifying before the defense even presents its case), but the only "surprise" should be the broker's testimony if he or she is called adverse—and that may add up to only one sleepless night when you must revise your direct outline to reflect the broker's testimony.

So, you are the expert informational filter for counsel. You must be careful in how that information is imparted— remember the caution about being too close to counsel and the team in that you must give all appearances of being an independent expert. You are, for the time being, a nobody in a hearing room. No visible reactions to testimony is permissible—none. Write down your epiphanies and get excited out of eyesight and earshot of arbitrators and the other side of the table. When you are sure that you to are alone, go ahead and give your insights and be assured that they will be appreciated since that is what the client is paying you for.

For now, your role is to be that filter and the source of opinions and insights.

**The Courtroom**

From an expert point of view, there are some significant differences between the arbitration room and the courtroom, but not all of them are relevant to the words that will come from the mouth of an expert.

Of course, the formality is the first thing that strikes any observer. Every courtroom is full of reminders that participants are engaged in a solemn ritual dating back to the founding of our republic. There are flags, a bailiff, a court reporter, a jury, the great deference paid to the judge, the melodious call to order, the act of rising when speaking, the formality of speech and of dress—but perhaps most importantly, there is the stringent rule of law which implies an absolute adherence to precedent and a slavish devotion to tradition.

In any courtroom in the United States, barring extraordinary events, anyone who is not a witness can observe the proceedings. This is contrary to an arbitration hearing where it is closed to observers. However, similar to an arbitration hearing, you, as an expert witness, can witness the proceedings. If counsel does not want you to participate full time, take advantage of this and observe the proceedings for a day, or at least a few hours, to get a feel for opposing counsel, the judge, the jury, and the tenor of the courtroom.

But because there may be a crowd in the courtroom (financial services trials being so riveting), and because of the ceremony that accompanies a civil trial, there is always the chance of intimidation. There is no need for intimidation; you are prepared to do your job as is everyone else who is a part of the trial, so simply concentrate on what needs to be done and do it.

There is also the issue of distraction as observers are free to come and go at will. Again, just concentrate on your testimony and the distractions will be unnoticeable.

When it comes to your testimony, the important difference between a trial and an arbitration hearing is that opposing counsel will know what you are about to say. He or she has had the opportunity to depose you, and you have, most likely, written an expert report, and therefore, your direct testimony should offer no surprises to the other side. This is especially true in federal court where expert reports are the norm. If there is something that escapes your lips that is foreign to opposing counsel; i.e., testimony regarding a topic which was not covered in your report, expect some low-grade fireworks. Opposing counsel will undoubtedly object, and rightly so, that he or she was denied the opportunity to examine the topic in your report and therefore also denied the opportunity to depose you on such topic. While there may be various rebuttals to such an objection, the objection will generally prevail, and there is nothing more to do than to move to another topic, one that had been previously disclosed.

When it comes time for cross-examination, expect your report to be the focal point; it was so on direct and even more so, it will be on cross-examination. Expect that your words on direct will be matched and catalogued with both your report and your deposition, and a multitude of questions will flow from even the slightest deviation between testimony and report and/or deposition. If slightly different words are used to describe the same issue between your direct testimony, your deposition, and your report, expect opposing counsel to discuss with you the variances in detail. If you meant no differentiation, say so and it will likely cut short the examination. If you wish to take the opportunity to clarify and select one word or phrase over another, that is fine, but expect a detailed cross-examination on the subject.

Also, be aware that if you and counsel agree that certain topics contained in your report will not be the subject of direct testimony, opposing counsel will be fascinated by the omission, and will certainly open a line of inquiry regarding that dog that is no longer barking.

Remember that in the U.S. federal court system, your report is generally not considered to be evidence; it is rarely entered as an exhibit. Most judges will not have read your report prior to your testimony even though it was available to the bench. The purpose of the report is to bind you into your opinions early, and to give opposing counsel a picture of your impending opinions. What does make a record, of course, is your testimony and the exhibits that reinforce that testimony.

However, whatever you do, do not take the opportunity on the witness stand, either on direct or on cross, to change your opinion. There is simply no reason to do so as you have had every opportunity to review the evidence, the exhibits, the depositions, and the opposing expert's report. There should be nothing in the testimony of fact witnesses that would alter your opinions since you have read the depositions of every key witness. The "out" you gave yourself when submitting your report, i.e., that you reserve the right to alter or supplement your opinion upon learning of newly discovered evidence, is operable, if at all, during the discovery phase of the trial, not at the trial itself.

The only possible reason to alter an opinion might be the game-changing deviating testimony of a fact witness which greatly and significantly diverges from a deposition upon which you relied. In that case, you may have to alter an opinion, but be prepared to discuss this with counsel in advance, and recognize that it will be fodder for extensive cross-examination. This will certainly not be a surprise to counsel who will also have been stunned by the testimony.

As previously noted, expect every substantive line of your report to be challenged on cross. Recall Essential Rule Number Twelve: "Every word of your expert report will be dissected; you must be prepared to be deposed and cross examined on every, and I mean every, word in your report." This is where you use the precision you have developed and are well prepared to go to battle with opposing counsel.

* * *

**A Personal Aside:** *I have long since forgotten the broader subject matter, but vividly recall the protracted BillClinton-esque cross-examination battle over the word "therefore." Whether I, by using the word, implied causation or not, and why it was omitted from one aspect of the testimonial record, kept the court reporter busy for a good half hour.*

The rules of evidence, while relaxed in an arbitration setting, are strictly enforced in court. You will be hearing objections such as "hearsay," and "asked and answered," "best evidence rule," and "relevance," among many others. Let the attorneys do their job and fight the evidentiary battles. Even if you are on the receiving end of an objection, it should not concern your substantive testimony. You have committed neither a sin nor a crime; it is only a procedural or technical matter. Just enjoy the respite and the repartee.

Perhaps the biggest difference between an arbitration hearing and a courtroom trial is your audience. As previously mentioned, in court, you are now addressing a jury and a judge—or perhaps only a judge—and therefore your testimony should take on a different tone than speaking to an arbitration panel. Review the sixth "Characteristic of a Successful Expert" found in Chapter 2: "Understand Your Audience." You must match your delivery, your pace, your depth, and your emphasis to match the level of comprehension of your audience. It will do you no good to dazzle a jury with your expertise if your words are incomprehensible to the average member of that jury.

Finally, a small point: in securities arbitration, the results of that arbitration are made known through an e-mail or facsimile sent by FINRA to counsel thirty (or more) days from the final date of the hearing. In some cases where post-arbitration briefs are required, the time-frame is considerably longer. Fair enough; that is how the system works. However, in court, expect a verdict on a same-day basis. The defense will rest, closing arguments are made, jury instructions given, and then deliberations will begin. Trials involving securities matters are not usually the type of cases where juries take days to decide or get deadlocked easily. It is some comfort to know that you can stick around (if you so choose) and receive the verdict shortly after the case concludes.

* * *

**A Personal Aside:** *In direct contravention of the above, I testified in a non-jury trial (also known as a "bench trial") in federal court in Chicago where the judge took in the evidence and told the parties that a verdict would be forthcoming shortly, but that the parties should not stay in the courtroom. Good advice. Seven months later, a partial verdict was rendered regarding liability, but not damages. Almost two years later, the verdict on damages was given. Sometimes, the exception may be the rule, and arbitration may be the swifter method.*

### The Mediation Room

Every so often, the services of an expert witness will be requested in a mediation. Consider yourself to have "arrived" when counsel requests your presence to present arguments to a mediator to bolster and embellish those of counsel.

Mediation is a voluntary arrangement wherein the parties agree to present their "case," i.e., their arguments, both factual and legal, to an impartial third party in lieu of, preceding, or in some instances, during, litigation or arbitration. The theory behind mediation is that such an independent voice will be able to facilitate an agreement between parties after hearing both sides of a dispute. The goal is settlement of the dispute, arrived at in a voluntarily (although not necessarily cordial) manner, which will end the matter and result in the dismissal of any litigation.

Mediation is a contractual procedure, with the terms

and conditions of the process set forth by the mediator. If successful, the plaintiff (or the complainant) will agree to a dismissal of the matter in return for whatever the parties agree to as a just resolution. Any money flow will go through the offices of the mediator to facilitate resolution and prevent any misunderstandings. Likewise, a mediator will be prepared with the appropriate paperwork to lay the foundation for an ultimate dismissal of a lawsuit and the same paperwork will state clearly the terms of the settlement which usually includes a non-disclosure provision.

In reality, mediation is a compromise; in a successful mediation, each side will invariably give up some key points, and therefore some bargaining power, despite each side believing strongly that their position is absolute and righteous. No one likes a compromise: if the Plaintiff strongly believes that he or she was damaged by $X Million, it hurts to settle for less. If the Defendant strongly believes that there was minimal liability, it galls the businessmen in the room to pay more than what was "penciled in." But for a mediation to be successful, by definition, both sides will be forced to compromise. Throughout the procedure, legal liability slowly diminishes as an issue and is replaced with the reality of dollar amounts to make the process end. The mental calculations on both sides turn to "How much will it cost to prosecute/defend this matter, and what is my (ever shifting) bottom line?" It is the mediator's job to work with both parties to pull those bottom lines together.

A good mediator will refuse to give up even when there is little movement, even after hours of shuttle diplomacy. A good mediator knows that a cooling-off period can sometimes bring results, and therefore will keep a mediation "open" even after one or both sides decide to "walk." Many a mediation turns from failure to success in the days or even weeks following what appears to be a fruitless day of talking.

Mediation is an all-day, or a multi-day affair. I have never participated in a mediation which took less than eight hours. It is held in a conference center, a law firm, or any other neutral site that has multiple meeting rooms—but it is not an adversarial proceeding. It is not one person or one side against the other. There is no judge, jury or arbitration panel. Rather, it is designed to achieve denouement—settlement—an end to a dispute.

Depending on the temperature of the parties, there may, or may not, be a joint introductory session wherein the ground rules are presented and opening statements are presented by the attorneys. If the level of hostility is too great, the mediator may decide that a joint session would be disadvantageous, and ground rules are presented by the mediator and opening statements presented by an attorney in a separate venue, one side only in a room.

From that point forward, regardless of the parties' emotional status, the sides are kept apart and the mediator shuttles between two rooms, hearing arguments, presenting suggestions, offering advice, telling each party (within the strict boundaries of confidentiality) the status of the opposing party, where a settlement might be achieved, and what creative ideas might be set forth. It is through this process, wherein the mediator plays the role of counselor, lawyer, psychologist, diplomat, and nudge, that a resolution might be forged.

The reality of having separate quarters means that there will be time, lots of time, hours of time, where the mediator is speaking to and cajoling the other side. One is left to do whatever otherwise needs to be done in those "off-hours" since the process is informal; i.e., there are no witnesses to prepare, no cross examination to finalize, no jury instructions to write. Truth be told, there are a lot of crossword puzzles filled in, lots of internet searches performed, and many newspapers read while the mediator is talking to the "other side."

The role of the expert in a mediation is that of an aide to the mediator; there are issues which are too complex to be dealt with by counsel alone, and the intricacies are there for the expert to explain to the mediator, virtually one on one. The mediator is not an expert in the nuances of a case: he or she might do several of these proceedings in any given week. Therefore, the expert is brought in to supplement counsel's arguments with the same type of exhibits that might be used at a trial or an arbitration and the explanation of those exhibits is critical to sway a mediator's thinking regarding the next steps to be taken.

●  ●  ●

**Note:** *Counsel will have a legitimate concern divulging to the other side exhibits which, in case of a failed mediation, might later be used at a trial or arbitration. The concern is that the element of surprise would be lost if the mediator uses the exhibits with the other side now in an attempt to show the strength of your case. ("Free discovery" is the term used by most counsel). However, this must be weighed against the real possibility that the expert documents could successfully end the mediation. Therefore, even if the expert documents are spot-on magnificent and would resonate well with any trier of fact, the use of those documents vis à vis not showing them to the other side must be discussed with the mediator.*

If you have been brought to a mediation, your job is to act as the expert that you certainly are. Do not play lawyer; use your knowledge and your skills to explain to the mediator, from your expert point of view, why counsel's arguments are solid. Use the documents that you have prepared to bolster those arguments. Explain them fully and well. Have a dialogue with the mediator; do not lecture, but in a conversational tone explain your point of view.

A good mediator will be eager to hear from you, essentially another third party, as to the strength of your lawyer's case. And if you are confident that your case is, in fact, strong, now is the time, under questioning by the mediator, to admit to any weaknesses as well. There is nothing so strong as the admission of certain non-critical weaknesses when asked a direct question.

A proficient expert put into this position is invaluable to a mediator. There have been numerous times when I was asked to confer with the opposing clients to show them what I might testify to if the matter is not settled during mediation. During those sessions, I would meet with the clients (and their attorneys) and give the same type of explanations that I gave to the mediators. Opposing counsel's reactions, of course, varied greatly, from intense interest, to hostility, to professed boredom. What was discussed between them after I left the room is, of course, unknown to me, but as the saying goes, I would have loved to have been a fly on the wall.

Occasionally, during the course of the back and forth, I would be asked to confer with the expert on the other side to see if there was mutual understanding of the differences which separated the parties. This informally mirrors the British system of letting the experts confer and produce areas of agreement and disagreement.

●  ●  ●

**A Personal Aside:** *In one memorable mediation in Boston I found myself opposite a good friend, an excellent expert of high integrity and knowledge. After hour upon hour of no apparent progress by the parties, he and I met at the coffee machine and took it upon ourselves to settle the case. It was a matter that clearly should be settled. We knew both sides' strengths and weaknesses, we knew the just and equitable dollar amounts, we knew the theories that would get us to that dollar amount. Therefore, we worked it out on paper, presented it to our respective attorneys and then jointly presented it to the mediator. Within thirty minutes thereafter, we were out the door with both sides claiming a successful mediation. It doesn't get any more satisfying than that.*

**Another Personal Aside:** *The success of a mediation often depends on the subject matter knowledge of the attorneys. If either attorney is not knowledgeable in the securities laws and practices, there is a great danger that the mediation will fail and the client not be well served. Such was the case in a mediation where the attorney representing our side, a claimant, was admittedly uninformed about the nuances of securities law and securities practices. Counsel was so ill prepared, that he turned to me just prior to his opening statement and said to me: "Please make the statement and you are now lead counsel on this matter." Shocked, I struggled through an opening statement, but then composed myself sufficiently to bring the mediation to a successful conclusion. It did help that, for reasons that will remain unspoken, our client was completely uninterested in the outcome, win, lose or draw.*

Being asked to participate in a mediation is a testimony to your reputation, your knowledge, your ability to communicate and your skill as an expert. If counsel raises the issue of attendance at a mediation, I would advise you to accept the honor and agree. If the issue of mediation is raised in the abstract, I would encourage you to raise with counsel the possibility of attending; good things can flow from that conversation.

# CHAPTER EIGHT

# TESTIMONY OF THE EXPERT WITNESS

## *Voir dire*

Generally, although certainly not always, the last person to testify on either side of the table is the expert witness which reflects the importance of that testimony. Expert testimony wraps up and summarizes the case; it is, in effect, a pre-closing argument because most, if not all, of the contested issues are dealt with by the expert. If you are testifying for the claimant, counsel will usually rest after your testimony is completed. If you are on defense, you will be the last witness heard by the arbitration panel and you have a unique opportunity to make an impression upon the panelists who will usually go into deliberations directly after closing arguments. Whichever side you represent, hearing, understanding, and critiquing the opposing expert is a critical component of your job.

Even in the arbitration setting, there is a bit of drama and ceremony regarding the qualification of the expert witness. Opposing counsel will take the introduction of an expert witness as an opportunity to question his or her qualifications to be an expert, either in general, or in the matter at hand.

In practical terms, it means that the very beginning of a proposed expert's direct examination will entail the submission of the C.V., followed by the expert's detailed testimony regarding his or her background. (Recall that you have practiced, practiced, practiced your background as it relates to this matter). Then, usually, but not always, the counsel who is presenting the expert witness will then ask the panel to "qualify" the witness as an expert in enumerated subject matters. Technically, this is not necessary; it is a nod to civil court proceedings where it is, in fact, necessary to qualify an expert. Nevertheless, most counsel make that request of an arbitration panel.

That request will trigger opposing counsel to rise and request "a few questions on *voir dire*." *Voir dire* is a French term meaning "to see; to speak" and the chair of the panel will undoubtedly grant the request, especially since there is generally no objection to that relatively standard request.

*Voir dire* has a multi-faceted intent:

First, *voir dire* is a legitimate attempt to examine the qualifications of the proposed expert to ascertain whether he or she should be given the deference that an expert, by definition, will be granted. During a hearing, his or her words will be taken seriously, they are cloaked with the expertise that the title "expert" endows them. Those words are intended to influence the outcome of the proceeding, and therefore, are considered by all parties to be most noteworthy. And so, the very C.V. that one worked so hard to perfect is dissected by counsel, through questioning of the proposed expert, line by line, job by job, accomplishment by accomplishment.

Counsel is rightly concerned that one who has **general** expertise may not have the **specialized** expertise demanded by the fact pattern which has evolved in the litigation before the panel. An expert in "securities" may not have the requisite knowledge or background of one who brings IPOs to the market, or who declares an emergency and halts trading on the floor of an exchange. An expert in retail sales may not have the requisite knowledge or understanding of the world of an RIA, a Registered Investment Advisor.

Qualifications are a legitimate concern when dealing with highly technical matters, and counsel has a right to explore, in depth, the credentials of any proposed expert who might offer damaging testimony against his or her client. Therefore, highly specialized questions, prepared well in advance, are flung at the proposed expert to test his or her expertise. Qualifications are examined not only in general, but in reference to the facts at issue and filtered against the witness's professional experience. The intention is to ascertain whether he or she is, in fact, qualified to testify; a determination upon which the panel must, upon motion, ultimately rule.

Second, *voir dire* is an attempt to ascertain, with specificity, what testimony is proposed to be given. Recall that there are generally no depositions in FINRA arbitrations, so counsel can only discern through the 20-day exchange on what topics an expert intends of opine. *Voir dire* is a devious, albeit it perfectly legitimate, way of learning which topics will soon be discussed. It gives counsel a "heads up" regarding the impending testimony while simultaneously asking questions regarding the witness's expertise on those topics. Cloaked in the innocent request to "Identify the topics to which you intend to opine," counsel now has a two-pronged strategy. If one or more of the topics is felt to be inappropriate for expert testimony, e.g., a purely legal presentation, there will be an immediate objection to that part of the proposed testimony and a motion (*"in limine"*) to exclude the offensive matter will be offered. Likewise, if a topic is proposed where no documentary materials were provided, counsel may object to the element of surprise.

Third, *voir dire* is, sadly, (and without political correctness), intended to rattle the proposed expert witness. If there are any technical errors in the CV, counsel will exploit them. If there are shortcomings in the background, either professional or personal, counsel will pounce upon them. If there is a mention, or a failure to mention, a disqualification or limitation of previous testimony by a court or an arbitration panel, it will be explored in detail. If there are trivial or semi-trivial deficiencies such as missing dates, missing duties, unclear responsibilities, too many job changes, not enough job changes, failures on exams, allegedly misleading statements or improper licensing—counsel will explore them in great depth, and generally not in the most kind and gentle manner.

Fourth, there is a hope that the expert witness will be disqualified from testifying, or limited in the areas upon which testimony will be taken. It is not a futile desire, as it happens, not frequently, but with some regularity. It used to be a "kiss of death" to have been limited or disqualified in a previous proceeding since it gave the panel implicit permission to do it again in any questionable situation. However, in recent years I have seen panels take a previous disqualification or limitation into consideration as just one of many factors. The more serious concern from the expert point of view is whether counsel will even consider hiring a proposed expert who has been limited or disqualified from testifying.

The job of the expert during his or her own *voir dire* echoes somewhat the earlier tips on cross-examination since it **is** cross-examination although on a more limited and personal level. The difference is that, in a practical sense, there will be no re-direct to save yourself if counsel begins scoring points on your qualification to testify. (Technically, your counsel can immediately follow up with re-direct after opposing counsel is done, but by then, the damage may have been done, so consider opposing counsel's questions your sole opportunity to set the record straight on the merits of your qualifications you detailed on your opening direct examination).

Therefore, although the same tips to be relaxed but alert, answer the questions with brevity, listen carefully to the premise of each and every question, be polite, and so forth still apply, I would tend to be more forceful in your own defense (but always maintaining your responses within the bounds of decorum). In this regard, do not let a negative allegation regarding your qualifications go unrebutted; do not accept an instruction to answer only "yes or no;" explain any nuance completely; correct counsel concerning any misrepresentations regarding your C.V.

Consider an aggressive *voir dire* to be an attack not only on your credibility and your qualifications, but on your very livelihood. If you followed Essential Rule Number Six ("No one should attempt to testify—or even consult—if there is even the slightest internal discomfort regarding one's expertise."), you know with absolute certainty and absolute confidence that you are fully qualified to testify. Your job on *voir dire* to make sure the panel also knows that to be true.

Following the *voir dire*, opposing counsel will do one of four things: "We accept Mr. Phileas Fogg as an expert," (whereupon Mr. Fogg now breathes easier), or "We move that the panel limit the testimony of Mr. Fogg to the following areas: XYZ," or conversely, "We move to exclude any testimony relating to ABC," or the ultimate petition, "We move to disqualify Mr. Fogg as an expert."

Before the panel decides on the motion, assuming you were not accepted as an expert by the other side, your counsel will, if necessary and as previously stated, have an opportunity to re-direct you to rehabilitate your savaged reputation. But truly, the onus is on you to create the positive impression on the *voir dire*, not on the re-direct. Nevertheless, counsel will, on such re-direct, point out your glorious accomplishments, how well credentialed you are, what a good dresser you are, how relevant and helpful your proposed testimony will be—and then once again request that you be qualified as an expert to testify on matters before the panel.

The panel will either take a short break and leave the room (better that three individuals depart than have the entire circus pack up and leave), or the three members will huddle quietly at the front and whisper in each other's ears. Reading the tea leaves is always risky, but the apparent keys, from experience, are: If the panel leaves the room, there is something substantive to discuss, either disqualification or limitation; if the panel huddles, it is not a close call, the expert will testify without limitations. Furthermore, if the break is more than ten minutes, it means either that there are very serious discussions being held—or a panel member has decided to use the restroom.

Following the break, the chairman will reconvene the hearing and announce a decision which is final and not appealable. So much for the preliminaries…

# CHAPTER NINE

# THE OPPOSING EXPERT TESTIMONY

*There is a Duty and it Falls on You*

Once the drama of *voir dire* is concluded, assuming there is no disqualification, the expert will be examined by counsel. Like any fact witness, the direct exam will be somewhat (or highly) scripted. Unlike a fact witness, the expert will give opinion testimony presumably backed by exhibits to visually and technically prove his or her various points.

Understanding and internalizing the testimony of the opposing expert and communicating your comments to counsel for purposes of assistance with the upcoming cross-examination is critical to your roll as the expert. Come out from the shadows of the back wall of the hearing room and sit next to counsel to hear your counterpart impart contrary or alternative wisdom.

**ESSENTIAL RULE NUMBER THIRTEEN: Critiquing the opposing expert is a critical job function. Counsel is relying on your expertise for an effective cross-examination. You have an implicit duty to relay to counsel your expert, in-depth analysis of the testimony and work product of the opposing expert.**

Your immediate job is listen with extraordinary care and to take detailed notes. Do not attempt to write down testimony word for word; you will just get bogged down in the trivia. Instead, develop a shorthand method. Take down the important points including any words that seem odd or out of place. Sometimes, you are not recording the testifier's words at all, but are highlighting thoughts that were triggered from testimony that you want to review with counsel. This is where you can be most valuable: **Others are transcribing mere words; try to think bigger-picture and add value by using your experience to raise critical questions about what everyone in the room is hearing.**

You already have an expectation of what will be said, perhaps even what should be said, because of the 20-day exchange. Now put those expectations to a critical test and hold them up to the testimony you are hearing. Is there something that surprises you? Why? Is it contradictory to something you received, or is it just nuance? Does it negate anything you received or enhance it? Does it create an opening that makes a document previously turned over incorrect or irrelevant? This is a crucial part of the hearing and you must think critically and precisely. Your antenna must be up and finely tuned.

* * *

**A Personal Aside:** *Over the years, I have vacillated between taking notes on a legal pad and using a laptop computer while attending a hearing. There is nothing wrong with bringing a computer into the hearing room; I have attended many a hearing where counsel and experts are all taking notes and referring to documents on a laptop. However, towards the end of my career, I settled on a hybrid method: I would have all* *the exhibits and other documents stored on my laptop and would refer to them when counsel is questioning a witness (or whenever I felt necessary to refresh my recollection), but I preferred to take notes in longhand where I can scribble annotations, draw lines between relevant points of testimony, or take down actual quotations. Either method is acceptable; experiment and see what works best for you.*

You will have some opportunity to review your notes with counsel since it is customary to allow counsel a short break before cross-examination begins in order to gather information, revise the outline of questions, and to talk to the client. The best-case scenario is that cross-examination is deferred until the next day, and you have the evening to plan strategy—but do not count on that; from experience, I can tell you that it rarely works out that way.

So, most likely, you will have a limited amount to time to express yourself to counsel before cross-examination begins. Organize your thoughts and emphasize your most important points. Remember, not all your points regarding the opposing expert may make it into counsel's cross-examination, but if you are on defense and have not yet testified, you will have the opportunity to testify to many or all the points on your own direct testimony.

Listening with "extraordinary care" triggers a duty, not in a legal sense, but in a professional sense. You must hear not only words, but you must dig deeper, open your mind and put your experience to work and consider it your **duty** to hear what no one else in the room hears. You must listen for the theories being proposed; i.e., listen for the big picture and try to square it with your theory of the case. You should have had a clue as to what the opposing theories are from the pleadings, the briefs, and the work- product exchange twenty days ago, but now try to internalize how the expert weaves the fact-witness testimony into his or her own testimony and the written work product. Ask yourself:

- Are the theories unique or novel?

- Are they plausible?

- Do they negate any other testimony?

- Do they fly in the face of any well-accepted treatises?

- If the theories are to be accepted by the panel, might those theories be stretching the boundaries of custom and practice in the industry or even laws, rules or regulations?

- If not stretching those boundaries, might they be outright inapplicable?

- Even if the theories are plausible, is there a valid reason to apply them to the facts in the matter before the panel or is there a more common or logical application?

- Are the theories consistent with what the written work product intends to prove? In some instances, one cannot have it both ways: The theory of the case leads in one direction while the presentation of exhibits will stray from that area into another dimension altogether.

- Looking for and analyzing the big picture is analogous to understanding the premise of a question on cross-examination: The threshold may be the problem and it must be carefully considered before moving on.

Listen for any implicit or explicit contradictions:

- Does the expert contradict himself or herself within the four corners of the testimony? This is where good notes are essential as you can point out to counsel exactly what was said in each instance and how and why both utterances cannot be true. Annotate your notes so that the connection between the statements is clear.

- Are there any statements made by the expert which contradict any testimony that you heard from fact witnesses during the hearing? The direct testimony may have been prepared days or even weeks ago, and now, after other testimony has been received, it may lie in contradiction to what the panel has heard.

- Are there any contradictions between the oral testimony and any written documentation presented by the expert during discovery? Always have work product in front of you and refer to it during the direct examination of the opposing expert. There is often a conflict between the spoken word and the written work product.

- Are there any hidden or implicit contradictions; i.e., if X were true, then Y, as stated, cannot also be true? Sometimes a statement will contradict a seemingly unrelated part of the case, but your job is to know the materials and the testimony so well that you can bring a hidden contraction to light.

Listen for key words. This is a legal proceeding where words matter, especially out of the mouth of an expert who presumably knows the jargon, the law, the industry rules, the customs and practices of the securities industry, and knows how to persuade a trier of fact. Therefore, there are trigger words to which you should be finely attuned. When used properly, there is a message being sent and you must receive it for what it is and be able to respond either during your own examination or to be given to counsel to be used on the opposing expert's cross-examination. If it is used improperly or carelessly, it is relevant and interesting fodder for expert cross-examination, and you should be the one to point it out to counsel.

For example, if the opposing expert uses the word "suitable," you must understand that it has a specific, defined definition within the industry. It is used casually with great peril, because it does have that industry-specific meaning, and improper use can lead to lengthy examination regarding what was really meant: "As an expert, are you aware of the legal meaning of the word?" Did you intend it to be used in the legal and industry sense?" "How do you define the word 'suitable'?"

Likewise, the word "recommend" triggers enumerated duties within the industry. There are several FINRA Notices to Members attempting define exactly what constitutes a "recommendation." Again, casual use of that word is dangerous and can rebound with adverse consequences.

Sometimes, an expert inadvertently plays at being a lawyer. Note those attempts, and be sure counsel is aware of them. For example, the words "negligent" or "negligence" are legal terms with specific meanings within the world of tort law. A layman who throws out those terms might have to undergo a cross-examination as to which specific duty was breached, what damages flowed from the breach and where the proximate cause could be found.

Likewise, interpreting caselaw, while generally not accepted as testimony by panels, will occasionally occur anyway. Counsel will make a pro-forma objection, but in more cases than not, counsel relishes the opportunity to cross examine a lay witness on the law. It is a perilous journey for the layman who probably has not fully researched the origins of the case as well as the subsequent cases which interpreted it. Nor, in most instances, do laymen grasp the complexities of a decision; e.g., the importance of footnotes in caselaw which can lay out the intricacies of the thought process of the presiding judge.

An expert may deliberately obfuscate a presentation with too much jargon. In my experience, this is a deliberate attempt to bolster the appearance of "expertise." But one who is now testifying as an expert has already been qualified as such; the expertise is not only a given, but is on the record. Trying to impress an arbitration panel with jargon is simply annoying and has never been a worthwhile strategy.

Determine whether the presentation of exhibits is fair, relevant, understandable, and unbiased. You may disagree as to the meaning or the interpretation of the data, that is understandable and somewhat expected, but any exhibit must present data that is absolutely neutral to be helpful to a panel. If it is not, if it reveals partiality, it reflects on the independence of both the expert and the presentation.

There should be nothing within the presentation that has not been already accepted as evidence by the panel. Experts should not be throwing new evidence into the mix without a foundation having been otherwise laid.

Remember, except in unusual circumstances, you will have 20 days to have examined the exhibits of the opposing expert. You will have had the time to ask yourself the critical questions below. You should have, you will have, gotten counsel on the phone well in advance and discussed the flaws in the exhibits so that counsel was fully prepared for his or her cross-examination. Specifically, look at the exhibits with a critical eye and ask yourself:

Are there flaws in the logic? Like an internal examination of the premise of a question, look for logical flaws in a chart, graph or table. Ask yourself if there are contrary conclusions which could be drawn if only X were considered. Then, mentally throw X into the equation. Or take Z out of the situation—perhaps it does not belong in the equation at all. Perhaps X or Z are fact issues that are in contention and that counsel, through a fact witness, not an expert should be making. Perhaps it is being slipped into evidence through the expert instead of fact-testimony. In other words, be skeptical of exhibits—they can be a great tool "for good or evil."

Other questions to ponder:

- Does the opposing expert move consistently from presentation to conclusion? Does that leap make logical sense?

- Do the exhibits in use conform to those which were turned over during discovery? If not, why were they changed, and is counsel aware of the change?

- Does the data support the conclusion?

- Have any exhibits that were turned over during discovery been omitted in the testimony? If so, why were they omitted? Perhaps a theory has been discarded. The "dog not barking" tells a story by itself.

* * *

**A Personal Aside:** *An expert presented a table representing values of various assets in a margin-liquidation matter but failed to identify with specificity the relevant dates and times of the valuations. Since the issue of valuation was critical to the actions of the respondents, the date and time of valuation was equally critical. During cross-examination, it was determined that the dates of valuation spanned a two-week period making the asset sums, as presented, virtually worthless for the purposes proposed.*

Are there flaws in the presentation which might lead to intended or unintended bias? In Chapter 2, under the fourth characteristic of an effective expert, I discussed the concept of a document being unintentionally misleading. Recall that one can be perfectly honorable, but the visual presentation or representation of data can be skewed depending on the method of display. Understand any pictorial representation of data, and therefore the conclusions that we draw from that representation, is highly dependent on how we see and internalize not necessarily the data itself, but the pictures drawn from that data. I try hard to look at the data, not the chart or the graph, and determine if there might be any unintended bias being presented to the panel. If there is, alert counsel as this is a relevant topic for cross-examination.

Are the exhibits, and thus also, the testimony which spawned the exhibits, relevant? This might be a point ultimately better made by counsel, but as an expert, you are there to assist counsel so you should be well attuned to the concept of relevance. Even if everything about the exhibit is fair, logically consistent, and free from presentation bias, it might be totally irrelevant and not pertinent to any point which relates to the issues at hand. The opposing expert may be raising issues under the cloak of expertise that should need no rebuttal because they are not pertinent. The exhibit may very well be the vehicle which allows testimony which, in a court of law, would never be admissible. Raise this issue with counsel so that the cross-examination can focus not on the details of the exhibit, but on the relevance of the broader picture and the subject matter itself.

Do I understand the exhibit well enough to be of assistance to counsel? When you first receive any exhibit, usually 20 days prior to the first date of the hearing, you should spend a great deal of time understanding the exhibits. Recall that exhibits, especially those that will be a visual part of opinion testimony, are a critical component of an expert's presentation.

If, after studying an exhibit at length, you cannot understand either the point of the exhibit or the methodology behind the exhibit, send an SOS to counsel. You and counsel cannot go into a hearing without a full understanding of the opposing expert's work, including the rationale behind the work.

Maybe the exhibit is flawed, logically chaotic, or it simply does not make any sense without footnotes or other explanatory material. Maybe it is simply incoherent. Maybe it is deliberately obscured to prevent you and counsel from understanding to what opposing expert will be opining. If after your best efforts, and that of counsel and the team of associates, comprehension of an exhibit remains a mystery, counsel has the option of requesting clarification from opposing counsel. There is no guarantee that cooperation will be given (short of appealing to the panel), but at least you and counsel are well-armed to be skeptical of this exhibit and the testimony that will be presented in its defense.

Does the work product of the opposing expert change any of my opinions? Is there something about those exhibits which makes me re-think my positions? Do I have an uneasy feeling in my stomach that the other side knows something that I did not know, or that they seized upon a relevant point that I overlooked or disregarded? Any one of those things are possible. Now deal with it.

- First, since you spent a great deal of time preparing your testimony and your exhibits, the chance that you overlooked a critical detail is small.

- Second, if the opposing expert does cause the proverbial light bulb to go on, and you truly feel that your testimony, as proposed, fails to incorporate that necessary point, it is not too late to weave it into your testimony. Yes, it might be too late for a new exhibit, but your testimony has not yet escaped your lips; you can incorporate it. You can certainly put a different "spin" on the same concept that your opposing expert will use. And worry not, you also need not use every exhibit of your own that was turned over. But first, look hard at the opposing exhibit. Are there flaws which do not relate to the concept you now wish to adopt? Is there any presentation bias? Can you use the concept but remain true to the remainder of your testimony?

- Third, it is rare, but there may be a time when that light bulb becomes a live and potentially deadly landmine which undermines your bed-

rock theories of your case. It happened to me
only once in over twenty years of testimony, but
it was indeed a killer. In such a case, you and
counsel will have to meet and regroup, rethink
your defenses and try not to wonder, at this point
in the process, what on earth happened. You still
may have twenty or so days to rethink strategy,
put together a new set of opinions, in essence,
create a new expert defense.

*       *       *

**A Personal Aside:** *My personal landmine was in the form
of deciding which statute should be deemed to be controlling
in the matter at hand: The Securities Exchange Act of 1934
or the Investment Advisor Act of 1940. Our entire defense
was predicated on the former. For various reasons (don't ask),
we did not consider the latter. The standards are completely
different as they relate to duties of a client representative
and once the two sides were on divergent paths, there was
essentially no recovery, no reconciliation. As a small bit solace,
unlike the situation described above, the exhibits turned over
to us did not tip us off as to the strategy of the other side; it
was first revealed during the hearing. But we should have
been prepared anyway. The panel bought logic of the other
side; we lost.*

Any references (whether appropriate or not) to manuals,
laws, case law, journal articles or anything else which can be
checked for accuracy and context are a priority for scrutiny.
Again, you should have seen them about twenty days ago,
and therefore, you will have had the opportunity for such
detailed scrutiny. Nothing that is presented by the other side

should surprise you. It is your duty to know when a statute was amended, when a rule was changed, when a section of a manual is out of date, when something was omitted from a citation, when there are numerous contrary articles which denigrate the opposing expert's presentation.

These are the types of aids that counsel needs from you to aid in cross-examination. Yes, some of this is also the function of counsel and his or her associates, but you must also capable of reading, reacting, and assisting counsel in countering the basis of opposing expert testimony.

Remember that on cross-examination, there is no need to turn over documents prior to the hearing. Therefore, you should be prepared to furnish counsel with any such materials for use during cross-examination well before the opposing expert testifies.

# CHAPTER ELEVEN

# THE FRUITS OF YOUR PREPARATION

## *Your Testimony*

How confident are you that you will be the expert that you hope to be? Of course, confidence is one of our "characteristics of the successful expert," but it does not just materialize; it is earned. And it is earned long before you enter the arbitration or court room, so let's take a step back and see how you and counsel prepared you for this day of testimony.

**First,** you did your homework and familiarized yourself with the big picture; the nature of litigation. Thus, among other things, you studied the:

* Nuts and bolts of a lawsuit;
* Meaning of pleadings;
* Order of testimony;
* Mechanics of a trial or an arbitration;
* Nature of a motion;
* Role of a fact-finder;
* Role of fact and expert witnesses;
* Meaning of opening and closing statements;

- Basic objections that counsel might be making;
- Role that the rules of evidence play.

You did this by researching those factors, by reading explanatory texts, or by talking to attorneys who practice litigation on a regular basis. It is your obligation to be familiar with the legal process so that you, and your work-product, can seamlessly fit into the remainder of the evidence. In this manner, you will not be (or look) bewildered when an attorney objects to a portion of your testimony; you will be part of the process and not an onlooker.

You need not be a litigation expert, but you will be an aid to counsel when you and your work-product, written or oral, fits well into counsel's grand scheme. And it will save counsel enormous amount of very precious time if he or she need not explain to you what opposing counsel meant by words such as "recusal," "redacted," or "hearsay."

**Essential Rule Number Fourteen** reads, in part: "**You are a part of a legal process and have an implicit duty to understand that process…**".

**Second**, you read and digested everything that was sent to you. You began with the pleadings. In fact, you may have had a hand in writing or reviewing either the Complaint (or Statement of Claim) or the Answer (or Statement of Answer). Likewise, you will have studied, in depth, the prehearing or pretrial briefs. You will have read these documents with great care (including the footnotes and citations), and internalized the positions of both parties as presented to the triers of fact. You now have the ability to take documentary and testimonial evidence and match it against the pleadings and the briefs to find both consistencies and inconsistencies. By recognizing the consistencies, you will have immersed yourself in the details of the litigation and have advanced your understanding of the matter. In recognizing the inconsistencies, you will be able to hold an intelligent and worthwhile discussion with counsel and attempt to ascertain any rationales for them. If no rationale exists for the inconsistencies, simply by pointing them out, you have already played a valuable role in the litigation.

**Third**, you took all documentary evidence that was time-specific and created a timeline of events. Consider all e-mails, any standardized form with a date stamp, all correspondence—anything that is correlated with a time, to be integral to the story that will be told, and thus, needs to be catalogued. Nothing in the evidence that is time-specific should be omitted. This timeline will be an enormous assistance in a complex matter where timing is critical.

Understand that some documents may have been withheld from you for strategic reasons; i.e., so that, for whatever reason, you could honestly say under oath that no, you had not reviewed that document. It could be that you might never know what was withheld. That is the best scenario since, on cross-examination, you can honestly say that no, you were not aware that the document existed. If counsel tells you that he or she prefers that you not see a document, accept that answer; do not push as to the reasoning, and understand that if asked on cross-examination why that document was not given to you, the answer is simply that counsel did not supply you with that document. The inevitable follow-up question is "Did you ask to see it?" The answer is "Yes, but counsel preferred that I not see the document." If there is fallout from that answer, it will fall, mostly, on counsel.

Everything else was reviewed, digested, and notes were

taken with an eye towards fitting each document into a possible "opinion-in-formation." By being so diligent, you can have the confidence that no document will surprise you. You can follow the testimony of other witnesses, actually being a step or two ahead since you know the timeline of events and the documents that support that timeline.

**Fourth**, you asked all the right questions of counsel, and of the key industry witnesses. Your questions probed the logic of your own opinions-in-formation and tested those opinions against the testimony that will be presented through fact witnesses. You cannot form opinions without a thorough understanding of the facts that will arise from a study of the materials and interviews, formal or informal. Probing counsel with difficult questions is both necessary and appreciated. Both parties benefit with questioning that tests theories and pushes pre-conceived concepts.

Do not simply accept counsel's interpretation of the facts; challenge counsel and you will be serving your intended purpose. You know enough about the facts, you are the expert in the operations of the securities markets and the broker dealer community, so rather than being a cheerleader for counsel's viewpoint, do yourself and counsel a favor and add to the discussion based on your experience. Counsel will be grateful for a learned individual (you) who can offer alternative theories, or who can say: "No, that just does not sound right based on industry norms." The discussion that then follows will be extraordinarily meaningful.

The same advice holds true for industry-witness preparation. I often requested to make special trips just to interview key out-of-town witnesses who are part of the industry—always accompanied by counsel either in person or telephonically. Whether you interview in person or on the telephone, you can add enormous benefit by talking to industry witnesses in their language; something counsel may, or may not, be able to do.

Urge counsel to allow you to talk to the key industry witnesses to assist in uncovering technical information or possible inconsistencies of which counsel may not be aware because the proper questions were never asked. Your assignment is to do an additional interview—the witness will have undoubtedly told his or her story more than once, far more than once—and use your in-depth industry knowledge as the focus. Ask tough questions, and extensive follow-up questions, especially If you get a sense that the witness is equivocating. In this moment, your assignment is not to make friends, but to assist counsel in evaluating the witness's story—which does indeed include the veracity of that story.

Following that interview, it is your responsibility to be absolutely candid with counsel regarding the veracity and the completeness of the story fashioned by the witness. It matters not a bit that you, counsel, and the witness are all "on the same side." If you smell the proverbial rat, or even just a small mouse, let counsel know your concerns. It is axiomatic that discrepancies are better discovered and dealt with sooner rather than later.

**Fifth**, you created exhibits from your opinions, transforming your words into visual representations. The creation of exhibits is both critical and difficult. It is a time-consuming effort that will pay enormous dividends, but must be done with extreme care as these exhibits will invariably be the subject of extensive cross-examination. If I did not have the technical skills either to work with the underlying data, or to create the visual, I found someone who could do so. Often, I would describe my hypothesis to a colleague more adept at either statistics or finance and he or she would work with me to determine if the data bore out the theory. If necessary, we would create alternative hypotheses and again test the data; that process could potentially go on for many, many cycles. Once we settled on a working theory that the data supported, I would turn to one or more colleagues who are adept at visual presentation to produce an exhibit that told our story clearly and professionally.

Clearly, not every point is made into an exhibit, nor is every exhibit noteworthy. Some of the most salient points are simply done verbally, and some of my exhibits were just tables of data; boring but necessary. It was up to me, and it will be up to you, to make a lifeless table come alive. That, dear expert, comes with practice.

**Sixth,** you worked carefully with counsel in crafting your direct examination. The extent of your involvement will vary from counsel to counsel and case to case, and will invariably grow as you gain experience. But my advice is to always be proactive. By the time it comes to preparing your outline of direct examination, you should have an excellent idea of what needs to be accomplished. You already know how to present your background, you will know what opinions need to be offered, and you will know which exhibits support them. You should also be proficient in references to other exhibits that could be useful to your testimony. That being true, why not offer counsel a rough outline of your testimony? Discuss it with him or her and perhaps you will be allowed to take the next step of creating the actual outline of your testimony to be used at the hearing. Even if you stop short of participating in the creation of the ultimate product, your contribution will be well received.

**Seventh**, you practiced your direct examination—again, and again, and again. We already noted the need to practice your **background** until it flowed flawlessly; the same is true regarding your **opinions**. And by "practice," I mean out loud. Lock yourself in your bedroom, bathroom, or bomb shelter and start talking. Every point must flow—not necessarily with perfect articulation, but every opinion must have a beginning, a middle, and an end. You should learn to make a point which will resonate with the trier of fact and that is done by reference not just to your spectacular background, but by reference to the facts, to the exhibits, to the pleadings, to the testimony that you heard. You must sell your opinions without a script, without memorization, which simply means you must know your topics perfectly. No, do not memorize a script which underlays the opinions and the discussion points behind the opinions, but you should be able to speak boundlessly on every point as if there were a script.

**Eighth**, you practiced your cross-examination. How? By anticipating the points of contention. You are perfectly aware of the theories anchoring the opinions on the other side of the table. You are also fully aware of the opinions that you are about to give which are contrary to your opponent's theories. Thus, you are aware of the points on which the other side will try to test you.

So, play opposing counsel and throw questions at yourself—scores and scores of questions: denigrate your own exhibits; challenge your own assumptions; sneer at your own qualifications; laugh at your opinions; ask for proof and sources on every point that you made on direct; look for any possible contradictions or weaknesses in your direct examination points.

Then do so on every exhibit and on every opinion. Following that exercise, turn it around and use opposing counsel's exhibits as if they were the gospel, and understand that those exhibits will be shown to you on cross-examination as being proper and correct. Ask yourself what is it about the opinions and documentation of the other side that is improper? Do you have the answers as to why your exhibits are pristine and the opposing ones are not? Do you have solid reasons as to why your theories are proper, and the opposing theories are not? They have experts with expert opinions, too. What is wrong with them? By playing opposing counsel, aloud, and practicing your answers to opposing counsel, it is astonishing how helpful that exercise becomes when faced with the real thing.

**Ninth**, you and counsel are well coordinated regarding your testimony, the timing of your testimony, your exhibits, the mechanics of the hearing, the relationship between your testimony and that of the other witnesses, the assistance expected of your regarding the opposing expert(s), and the annoying mechanics of billing and attendance expectations.

You have long since secured, and coordinated with counsel, the necessary but aggravating aspects of life on the road: air and hotel reservations, a rental car if necessary, a flexible return date. You have discussed when your first meeting time and place will be, and what is expected of you the night before the first hearing date. In other words, you can put those annoying mechanics aside and concentrate on the job at hand.

And so, with all the above preparation, it is your turn to testify. Advice on your testimony is a compilation of everything that has come before this section. Your testimony will encompass all eleven characteristics contained in Chapter

Two: Characteristics of a Successful Expert. Your testimony will be determinative when you are able to emulate those eleven characteristics. Your testimony will be flawless when you are able to present your credentials as if you have done it a thousand times.

You will shine when you are confident in your *voir dire*, when you have presented a professional expert report, and when you have given a near perfect deposition. You will be supremely confident in your cross-examination responses, having studied all eighteen keys to cross-examination survival found in Chapter Two of this book.

You will be clear and concise in your answers to both your counsel and opposing counsel. You can answer any question with precision regarding the exhibits you prepared, the derivation of the data, and the meaning of that data. You will have worked hard on your direct testimony with counsel to incorporate your opinions, formulated with care from the evidence presented to you during the discovery phase of the litigation. You will deliver that testimony with confidence, without arrogance, and not from memory, although you have indeed memorized the key points.

You will remember to fiercely guard your independence since you understand that the key to your longevity is your integrity. You will tailor your testimony to your audience, keeping in mind the varying levels of sophistication of the triers of fact. In that vein, you can be pedantic, you are, after all, a teacher, but never be too pedantic, since that might very well imply that you are talking down to your audience.

You will be candid, respectful, never prevaricate, never lie, never guess at an answer, while always listening with extraordinary precision to the questions given to you.

Finally, you will remember that one of your key functions is to aid counsel in analyzing the work and the words of the opposing expert. You and the opposing expert speak the same language; counsel may not. Therefore, you are the essential translator and your job begins the minute the other side turns over materials from the expert for your examination and continues during your direct examination which will include a detailed critique of the other expert.

**Tenth,** you gave reasonable deference to counsel. It is counsel's lawsuit to bring or defend, not yours. You are an important cog in that wheel, but counsel has every right to alter some of the "rules" that have been set forth herein. For example, I prefer to talk directly to a jury in order to better "connect" with them. However, your counsel may feel that looking and speaking to the questioner, the judge, or the arbitration panel, is preferable. Be flexible on those matters and on all of counsel's preferences save that of your honesty and independence. In fact, the entirely of **Essential Rule Number Fourteen** reads: "You are a part of a legal process and have an implicit duty to understand that process **which includes reasonable deference to your counsel's preferences**."

# CHAPTER TWELVE

# CONCLUSION

Anytime an individual proposes a roadmap to success, it is, by definition, perilous, and might also appear to be a bit pretentious. I never intended this book to be such. Hopefully, it reflects the best advice that I can give to a new or aspiring expert based on my experience in the field. Hopefully it will prove useful.

That "field" we usually refer to as one of being an "expert witness," but it is much more. It is really the alternative nomenclature, one that I greatly prefer, of "litigation support," since that is truly what you will be offering. Taking the witness stand is the cumulation of weeks or months of interaction with counsel in forming and shaping a complex legal case in the dispute resolution arena. Without question, it is what happens in the months preceding counsel's opening statement that is most critical; as crucial as the words emanating from your mouth during your testimony. Without your litigation support, there would be no expertise to wrap up counsel's presentation, the triers of fact would be deprived of the visual aids so necessary to drive home a point, and there would be no context for the often specialized, complex, and perplexing nuances of financial services. It is litigation support in the truest sense.

Some of the advice may be obvious (for goodness sake,

"speak clearly?"), but in context, even the obvious advice is a component of what goes into an effective career. Please trust me when I say that I have seen the obvious or the trivial (including "speak clearly") play a role in effective presentations. I have witnessed every example, and every line of this book is born from expert excellence or expert failings. My hope is that you will fall into the former category of expert excellence.

I began my career in the litigation support field knowing nothing. I believed, or hoped, that a position as a consultant in litigation support and as an expert witness would be a steppingstone to another position in the financial services industry. My goal was to stay at my firm for two or three years until something better or more interesting came along. It never did. The role of the expert witness is fascinating. You will meet the most captivating individuals, both attorneys and laymen. If you are lucky, as was I, you will have the pleasure of dealing with colleagues both talented and enthusiastic. You will deal with different issues, or nuances of similar issues, with every new assignment—and that variety keeps you enthused and eager. You will be well-compensated for your knowledge and your skills, and if you give fair value to your clients, your career can be long and very rewarding.

Good luck.

Portland, Oregon
October, 2018